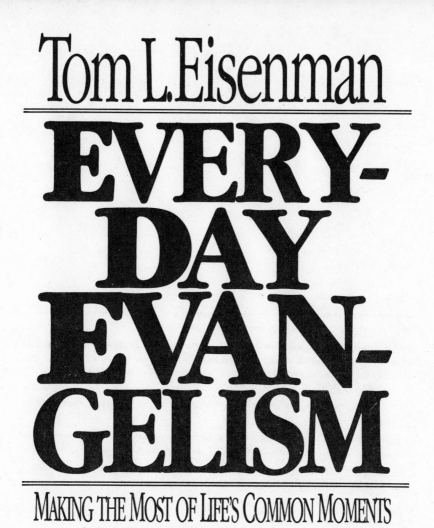

Tom L. Eisenman

EVERY-DAY EVAN-GELISM

MAKING THE MOST OF LIFE'S COMMON MOMENTS

*With Study Questions for
Individuals or Groups*

INTERVARSITY PRESS
DOWNERS GROVE, ILLINOIS 60515

InterVarsity Press is the book-publishing division of InterVarsity Christian Fellowship, a student movement active on campus at hundreds of universities, colleges and schools of nursing. For information about local and regional activities, write Public Relations Dept., InterVarsity Christian Fellowship, 6400 Schroeder Rd., P.O. Box 7895, Madison, WI 53707-7895.

Distributed in Canada through InterVarsity Press, 860 Denison St., Unit 3, Markham, Ontario L3R 4H1, Canada.

All Scripture quotations, unless otherwise indicated, are from the Holy Bible, New International Version. Copyrighted 1973, 1978, International Bible Society. Used by permission of Zondervan Bible Publishers.

Cover photograph: Michael Goss

ISBNs 0-8308-1703-4 (hardback)
0-87784-997-8 (paperback)

Printed in the United States of America

Library of Congress Cataloging in Publication Data

Eisenman, Tom.
  Everyday evangelism.

  "With study questions for individuals or groups."
  Bibliography: p.
    1. Evangelistic work.   2. Witness bearing
(Christianity)   I. Title.
BV3790.E36   1987   248'.5   87-3062
ISBN 0-8308-1703-4
ISBN 0-87784-997-8 (pbk.)

17 16 15 14 13 12 11 10 9 8 7 6 5 4 3 2 1
99 98 97 96 95 94 93 92 91 90 89 88 87

To Judie, whose living
and growing faith in Christ
and generous love for me
have been the rock
and reality behind the writing
of this book,
and to
Jana, Joshua, Jason and Gabriel,
with love.

Introduction: I Was Furious

I *was furious.* The store wouldn't take the defective fan motor back because I'd had it over thirty days. That meant finding a box, wrapping the motor, sending it off to the factory and going without the new ceiling fan for who knows how long.

And wait I did! One month, two months, and after nearly three months I called long distance. I reached a totally different company. Then the operator told me she could find no listing for the fan motor factory under the name I was giving her. I jumped in the car and headed for the store. They were going to get a piece of my mind.

On the way, though, something extraordinary happened. The Lord intervened. It was simple but profound. How should a Christian act in a situation like this? If a Christian is supposed to love his enemy, shouldn't he love a store manager too, even when there is a problem over defective merchandise?

My inner thoughts and emotions began to change. A moment

earlier I had been applying my creative energy to thinking of ways to beat the store. How about picketing on Saturday morning? Or maybe, if I had the old motor, buying a new fan, switching motors and returning it within the thirty-day warranty period.

But suddenly, a whole new world opened up for me. What might happen if instead of righteous anger I displayed cooperative grace? What if I could be more concerned about the hassle the manager was having in trying to get my problem solved than I was about my own hassle? Could I witness the love of Christ in this situation rather than short-tempered irritation?

It was amazing. No, my problem didn't go away. The factory first returned my old motor without repairing it. Then they sent a second motor that was assembled improperly. The third time they sent a good motor but it was for another model of fan. And finally the store manager gave me a new motor from a fan he had in stock, which is what I had asked him to do in the first place. No, the problem didn't go away, but the relationships I formed with the people at the store became real and fruitful.

Each time I returned to live out another chapter in our fan motor episode, I was congenial and tried as much as possible to understand what *they* were going through. Several times different people in the store thanked me for my understanding and patience. What good would it have done me to rant and rave? My anger would only have contributed to their defensiveness, and nothing positive would have been accomplished. The key was, they knew I had every right to be angry, but I chose instead to be gracious, and this made a difference.

Every time I see the young woman who most often worked with me to get the problem straightened out, she talks to me as if we were old friends. I know God can use this kind of positive relationship building as a way for non-Christians to contact the love and good news of Christ. Hundreds, even thousands of Christians take defective merchandise back to stores every day. What would happen if in each case the store clerks and managers were treated with extraordinary kindness and understanding? And this is just one small example of how Christians might take advantage of a common situation in contemporary culture to step into the lives of others with the love of Christ. It was the fan motor episode that started my thinking about the topic for this book.

I remember seeing at about the same time a human interest story on a major Denver TV newscast. They showed a young airplane mechanic stopping on the freeway to help a stranded motorist. This young man takes one evening a week to cruise the freeways in Denver with his tools, antifreeze and oil, helping every motorist whose car has broken down.

During the interview they asked him why he decided to be a good Samaritan. He explained that he was a Christian, and that the Bible said Christians were to love others or they had a dead faith. He said, "Some people can preach and some people can teach, but this is something I can do."

Two important things struck me as I listened to this young Christian man. First, he showed a real and practical understanding of the essence of the Christian's call to be an ambassador for Christ. Second, he had taken a good look at our contemporary society and identified a need that he could help meet with his gifts.

Most of us know what we're called to do and to be as Christians. But I'm sure that many make my mistake of not looking perceptively enough at the unique aspects of our modern society which may open new doors for Christians to witness Christ to the world. Hundreds of Christians must drive on Denver freeways every day. But only one, it appears, was driving with his eyes and his heart open. One young man saw in a truly modern problem—stranded motorists everywhere on the freeways—an opportunity to administer the practical love of Jesus to those in need.

I stopped for a moment to consider why a major Denver station would air a piece about the simple devotion of this young Christian man. But it makes sense. The world today is a tough place. People are in pain. People live in fear. Much of what contemporary society hands out to the average person is dehumanizing, depressing and debilitating. People are used, abused and discarded. Everybody is banged up. Nobody knows which way to turn. The point is, things have gotten so bad that even the simplest acts of love and caring today have become *big news*.

This should be a tremendous encouragement to us in the church. We are living in a day when the normal Christian person can make a huge contribution for Christ with even a moderate investment of love and kindness. Just a touch of love today can turn the world upside-down for Christ.

The opportunities are everywhere around us. People are hungry for love. If we pray and listen, God can open our eyes. We can see our common experience freshly. We can become acutely aware of how the gospel can minister to the needs of those around us. Instead of just living out dull patterns of activity, we can see each waking moment as a new opportunity to represent Christ in the world. This is the excitement of the Christian call, participating fully in the lives of others and seeing them changed through the power and influence of practical love.

This is a book about evangelism. But it is not a book on technique. It is a book about seeing in a new way. Each chapter attempts a new look at some common element woven into the fabric of our everyday lives. The topic, though, is open-ended. It is as infinite as the number of individual Christians, times the number of their gifts, times the number of contemporary situations of need that surround them.

Think of the impact we can have on those around us if we learn to see new open doors for the gospel in our neighborhoods, in our families, in our businesses, at our jobs, in all our relationships with others. Stepping into this way of seeing is the beginning of an exciting personal adventure in Christian living that never ends.

One young man discovered a place of effective ministry on the freeways of Denver. And then there he was, before a million TV viewers, talking about how important it is for him to live out his faith in Jesus.

What will it be for you?

1
Salvation Appeal

A *young woman came to talk with me one day about* joining the leadership development class I was starting in our congregation.

When I asked her about how she became a Christian, she told me an interesting story. She said that she came to the University of Colorado out of high school, and when she arrived in Boulder she needed to find part-time work. Her first job was waiting tables at the Boulder Country Club.

Out of all the people she waited on regularly, there was one couple who consistently treated her differently. They always engaged her in conversation, asking her questions about herself and her family. They were concerned about how she was getting along during her first year away from home. They communicated real interest in her.

After finding out that they were members of our congregation, she dropped in to worship one Sunday morning. It was just what she needed. The Lord did his work. In a few weeks she was in a new member's class, and soon she decided to follow Christ.

The couple she told me about have what I like to call salvation appeal. There is something about who they are and what they do that draws unbelievers to Christ.

The church is the people of God. Everywhere God's people go, the church goes. The church's mission is to represent the kingdom of God in the world. Paul proclaims the great mandate for the church when he writes, ". . . in Christ God was reconciling the world to himself, not counting their trespasses against them, and entrusting to us the message of reconciliation. So we are ambassadors for Christ, God making his appeal through us" (2 Cor 5:19-20 RSV).

This means that you and I are authorized representatives of the kingdom of God on temporary assignment in the world. God wants to use you and me to get his message across. He will make his appeal of love through us to those who need to know the love of Jesus Christ.

Christians should have salvation appeal. There should be something about them and about their loving action in the world that draws people to God. Paul describes earlier in 2 Corinthians this essential appealing nature of the Christian when he writes, "But thanks be to God, who always leads us in triumphal procession in Christ and through us spreads everywhere the fragrance of the knowledge of him. For we are to God the aroma of Christ among those who are being saved . . ." (2 Cor 2:14-15).

The couple who were members of God's church first, and the Boulder Country Club second, certainly were appealing Christians who for at least one young student became the aroma of Christ.

We can tell a lot about people by the aromas that accompany them. People who work in a garage or a kennel or who spend most of their time in a restaurant or who work with lumber all day or in a flower shop or in a health club or a dentist's office or butcher shop are often easy to spot.

The truth is, we carry with us in a number of subtle ways the environment in which we spend most of our time. If, then, we live our lives in God, close to him, spending our time with him in prayer and in study, fellowshiping with his people, we can expect to carry with us the aroma of Christ. This aroma will be the very fragrance of new life and sacrificial love. All Christians should want it, pray for it and work to have it.

There are three marks of being and acting that are the normal ways Christians become the aroma of Christ to unbelievers. They are the marks of the Master, and when they are found in his disciples, his reconciling work is accomplished in the world. Jesus had a singular purpose, a focused other-centered attitude and an astonishingly different approach in responding to those he encountered. This is what set him apart to accomplish his ministry. We too can learn these basics of purpose, attitude and action. They can make us more appealing Christians and help us to better accomplish our work of sharing Christ's message of reconciliation with the world.

A Singular Purpose

Jesus came to lay down his life for others. It is as simple as that. The Gospel of Mark spells it out in Jesus' own words, ". . . and whoever wants to be first [among you] must be slave of all. For even the Son of Man did not come to be served, but to serve, and to give his life as a ransom for many" (Mk 10:44-45). This verse makes two things clear. First, Jesus came to serve. Second, and this is not the same thing, Jesus did not come to be served.

The desire to be served rather than to serve beats in the heart of the world. The verse quoted above comes near the end of the passage where the disciples are in bitter argument about who will be granted the chief places in the kingdom. Jesus rebukes them for acting like the gentile rulers. They cannot be effective in kingdom work if they smell more like the world than the king.

If we want to be the aroma of Christ to the world, we cannot make the mistake of the apostles. If our life purpose centers on our desire to be served or to be ministered to (as some translations have it), we will represent the world's purposes, not the Lord's. But if the desire of our hearts can be changed through the power of the Spirit to conform to the single purpose of Jesus, we will be the aroma of Christ to the world.

Christians who easily become argumentative, angry, bitter, indignant, who lack joy and peace, can find in this transforming verse the key to a new way of living.

Think of the last time you were upset and angry about something. Perhaps you extended yourself to someone in love. You served another in a costly way. And then your service was not appreciated as you thought it should be. You expected more thanks. Now you wish you hadn't helped in the first place. After all, there are better things you could have done with your time.

What is the problem here? Is it that you came to serve another and the opportunity to serve was closed to you? Or did you come with a desire to be served yourself, to be thought of as kind and generous, to be ministered to by the thanks and praise of another? The truth is, if we hold an inner expectation to be served by others, we will often be disappointed. This is what causes our anger and indignation and our loss of Christian joy. But if our true purpose is to lay our lives down in service to others, we cannot be disappointed.

Recently a woman from another congregation asked me to speak at a district conference she was arranging. I found out in talking with her that her first-choice speaker had backed out on her at the last minute and that others she called before calling me were not able to do it. I was her frantic, last-hope choice.

I felt myself becoming irritated as I talked with her. I was just about to refuse to help when I thought about this principle of serving others first. Why was I feeling anger? Was it because I didn't think I would have anything of worth to offer at the conference? Was it because I didn't think I would be able to serve those attending the event or to serve this frantic woman calling on me to help? No, I was angry because I had not been chosen first. My feelings were hurt. I was not as high on her list as I thought I should be. Deep down, I had a desire to be ministered to, rather than a single purpose and life focus to minister to others.

I think of another time a few years ago when I worked with a new staff member to organize an important church retreat. I chose to make the new staff person visible at the retreat so he would be more widely and quickly accepted by the congregation. During the closing moments of the weekend, one person stood up and praised the other man's work of organizing and holding the retreat. My friend received a standing ovation. My inner reaction was not godly. Why? Was it because my plan to make him more visible to the congregation had failed? Or had I failed to make the retreat effective or to help those attending? No. I was not recognized. That was hard to take.

Think of the last time you felt you were overlooked. What was your reaction? Did someone else get a raise at work? Has a new person been placed ahead of you at your job or in church work? Has someone recently succeeded in an area in which you had previously failed? Or how about the last time you felt you had expertise but you weren't asked to contribute? The list could go on and on. In any case, if our life focus is to minister to others rather than to be ministered to, we can experience any of these things and still live in joy. But if we desire instead to be ministered to, we will often find ourselves frustrated, angry and without peace.

If we come into every life situation with one purpose only, to serve, wanting only to lay our lives down for others, we can never be disappointed. We can be glad for those who move ahead of us because the most important thing for us is that others have success. Jesus gave his own life so that we who deserved nothing could have everything there is, now and in the life to come.

This is the first major aspect of the aroma of Christ in the world. By making service to others our highest priority, we will become appealing people. When others benefit from our actions, we will have a deep inner satisfaction that we are accomplishing the work of Christ, and our true joy for others will be communicated. We will not be hurt if others get the credit; in fact, we will want others to receive credit, and we will rejoice with them when they are recognized. We will serve unselfishly without secret desire for consolation. In short, we will be laying down our lives for others with no expectations for ourselves. We will gain the inner "peace of God, which transcends all understanding" (Phil 4:7). And we will clearly communicate our practical love for everyone around us.

A New Way of Seeing

Jesus also demonstrated a tremendous capacity for recognizing and responding to human need. In the first chapter of Mark, verses 21 through 24, the narrative describes a day in the life of Jesus. He teaches with authority in the synagogue at Capernaum. There he becomes aware of a man with an unclean spirit. He commands the evil spirit to leave the man. Then he and the disciples go to Simon and Andrew's house where Jesus finds Simon's mother-in-law sick with fever. He heals the woman who then gets up and serves them. In the evening people from all around bring their sick to Jesus. He has compassion on them and heals their infirmities.

This text shows us that along with his single purpose in life Jesus also had an intense, *other-centered* attitude. He had an eye for the needs of people in the world around him. It may seem strange, but many Christians today are thoroughly dedicated to serving others but are somehow blind to the real needs of those who share their life circle. To be Christians who are the aroma of Christ to a hurting world, we will also need to develop our perceptiveness to the needs of those people Christ brings into our lives.

One important element in recognizing and responding to human need is making the time to be available to others. If we spend our lives rushing from one activity to another, we will not have the essential relaxed time to spend with others, to hear them express themselves, to learn about and respond to their needs. We also need to have time to be with God, to hear him speak to us about the people in our lives.

Jesus was very busy. The one day Mark described was as busy as the busiest days in our lives. But Jesus made time for the individual. He taught in the synagogue but ministered to the possessed man. He took the time to touch Simon's mother-in-law. He spent his evening hours ministering to the sick.

How does someone keep this kind of schedule without losing perspective in life? A key for Jesus was his quality time with the Father. After describing that incredible, people-filled day, Mark writes, "Very early in the morning, while it was still dark, Jesus got up, left the house and went off to a solitary place, where he prayed" (Mk 1:35). This is where we too will find our ministry guided by God, our energy restored, so that we can be fully engaged in life and responsive to the human need around us.

The story of the good Samaritan is an example of how the perceptive person will see and meet human need. You remember that a man was beaten by robbers and left to die at the side of the road. A priest and a Levite both passed the man. Obviously they could not stop to help. They were too busy doing the Lord's work. This is the blindness that can strike any of us if we're not on our guard. Finally, the Samaritan came by. He risked personal danger and made time in his schedule to help the fallen man. The Good Samaritan was an appealing person, showing the love of God to his neighbor. Think of the effect it must have had on this fallen man, waking up the next morning in a bed in an inn, to know that someone had not only stopped for him but also paid the bill for his care until he could make it on his own.

Perceptive Christian men and women will make time for others. When Paul says in Philippians 2:3, "in humility consider others better than yourselves," he is urging us toward a new awareness. We are to be *other*-focused. It is because we think so highly of ourselves that we spend so much time and energy on ourselves. If we can begin to think less highly of ourselves and more highly of others, we will find it easy to dedicate more of our time and energy to meeting the needs of others instead of our own. We will truly begin to see with the eyes of Jesus, and more often respond to human need as he responded, with costly and energetic love. If we are too busy to let others into our lives, to attend to them and to their concerns, sorrows, interests and joys, then we are too busy.

Throughout this book we will study this process of learning to see the world around us with the eyes of Christ. We can match a new attitude toward others with a new and singular purpose for our lives. We will see with Christlike awareness into the lives of those around us and be dedicated to serving them, laying down our lives to meet them with the practical love of Christ.

But there is still one more thing.

Second-Mile Living

Jesus taught second-mile living. This calls for creative Christian thinking and acting.

Second-mile living and loving is learning to do the unexpected, the unusually costly or thoughtful thing. For the Christian this will mean acting in a way that is contrary to the normal worldly response. Acting in this way toward others causes them to stop and think about the experience they have had. When Christians do the startlingly unusual thing for someone else and do it with genuine caring, the act is like a direct gift from God to the person who receives it.

Jesus said, "If someone strikes you on the right cheek, turn to him the other also. And if someone wants to sue you and take your tunic, let him have your cloak as well. If someone forces you to go one mile, go with him two miles" (Mt 5:39-41). This is second-mile thinking and acting.

The Christian life is filled with joy, suspense and continual surprise for the committed person who is open to the needs of others, dedicated to serve and thinking creatively about how to meet those needs with style and grace.

I remember a story a Chinese evangelist told about a Christian farmer who had to carry water to his rice paddy during the dry season. His paddy was separated from his neighbor's paddy by a dike and a water gate. The farmer carried water all day to his rice paddy. The next morning he discovered that his neighbor had raised the water gate during the night and let the water run down into his own dry paddy. So the farmer carried water from dawn to dusk again to flood his rice. Then, on the second morning, like the first, he found his own paddy drained and dry and his neighbor's well soaked. So on the third day, the farmer first carried water to his neighbor's paddy. Not until after it was well watered did he carry water to his own. This second-mile deed so struck the farmer's neighbor that he later became a Christian because of it.

I was moved a while ago by something David did. This ninth-grade boy in our youth program was big for his age, athletic and very tough, but he had a heart for Jesus. In school he was making a coffee table for his mother as a Christmas gift. He finished the table a few days before Christmas and left it in the shop so he wouldn't have to take it home and hide it. On the last day of school before vacation David went to pick up his table. He was shocked to find that someone had stolen it.

Now David was popular and had many friends. It did not take him long to find out who took the table. It was a younger boy who was unpopular and frail. So what did David do? He spent his entire Christmas vacation in the shop at school making a duplicate table. When he had it finished, he went to the other boy's house. When the younger boy answered the door and saw David standing there, he was petrified with fear. But David just said, "I have something I'd like to give you and your family for Christmas." He handed him the new table.

The younger boy burst into tears. He went into the house and came back with David's first table. The boys talked. The younger boy asked forgiveness, and David granted it. Within a few weeks the younger boy was attending the youth program at the church and eventually he became a Christian.

Second-mile livers and lovers are the aroma of Christ to those who are being saved. In both stories all three elements of salvation appeal are present. There is a deep dedication to serve in Christ's name and for his sake, with no concern about being served or ministered to by others. This frees the person from anger or bitterness that can create a consuming self-focus and hinder the process of creative need-meeting. In both cases there is a deep sensitivity to the real need in the other person's life and a willingness to make time to meet that need. And in both cases the Christians responded by living out the theology of the second mile. This kind of caring behavior is so incredibly unusual in our world today that it can have an enormous, life-changing effect on the person who encounters it.

This is how we were changed. We came to know what it cost for Jesus to leave heaven and come into our world, to live here among us and to die for us. He gave up everything that rightfully belonged to him so that we could have his rich blessings ourselves. Knowing this kind of love drew us to Jesus. The cross is God's second-mile thinking and acting on our behalf.

Jesus' appealing selflessness marked him. His constant, sacrificial love in action attracted us to him and still draws us closer each day. The more we know of him, the more we want to be near him.

These are the same appealing characteristics that should mark us as Christian disciples. The more our neighbors know us, the more they should want to be near us. And when they find out that we live and think and love the way we do because we follow the one who lived the perfect life of love, they will want to learn of him and follow him too.

By the power of the spirit and through prayer and attentiveness, we can learn to live our lives after the pattern of Jesus, at the very edge of love. The more we learn this, the more we will live in joy. For we will truly be living out the heart of our Christian call to be ambassadors for Christ. We can daily be the aroma of Christ to those who are being saved.

For Individuals or Groups

1. In the introduction, why does the author say our world is ripe for relational evangelism?

2. Do you agree with his analysis? Why or why not?

If so, discuss the signs of our times that you are aware of which support the author's view.

3. Describe in your own words what the author means in chapter one when he says that a Christian can have salvation appeal.

4. Think of someone you have known whom you believe has salvation appeal. What are the qualities that make this person appealing in Christ?

5. Name and summarize the three distinctive ways that Jesus loved those around him.

6. Think of one practical step you could take today in each of these areas—purpose (serving), seeing needs and second-mile living—which would help you to move toward greater effectiveness as an ambassador of Christ in the world.

2
The Risk of Love

My wife, Judie, was in Phoenix recently where she read a newspaper account about a woman and her little girl who were attacked by a man in a mall parking lot.

The big man approached the woman, grabbed her little girl from her, and said, "You can have other kids, lady. This one's mine!" Then he turned and rushed away between the cars with the woman's daughter in his arms.

The lady first screamed for help. No one responded. So she ran after the man. She caught up with him and started struggling with him, continuing to scream for help.

By this time there was a large crowd gathering. But still no one came to her aid. The woman managed to wrestle her child away from the man. She dropped her little girl to the pavement and lay down on top of her, holding her tightly to protect her. Instead of running away, the man began beating the woman and kicking her in the sides and back, all of this in front of a large crowd of people who stood and watched and never lifted a finger. After some time, the man pushed his way through the crowd and disappeared.

The sad thing is, there had to be Christian men and women in that crowd of observers. In a group that size there must have been many who claimed to believe in Christ. But not one would come forward to help this woman.

A Sign of the Times

Apathy, the refusal to risk involvement, is a prevalent sign of our times. As far back as March 1964 the nation was shocked into awareness of this fact when *The New York Times* reported, "For more than half an hour, 38 respectable, law-abiding citizens in Queens watched a killer stalk and stab a woman in three separate attacks in Kew Gardens."[1] Not one of those witnesses even called the police.

Our nation was shocked and horrified again more recently when a young mother of two in New Bedford, Mass., was raped repeatedly for over an hour in a public tavern. *Newsweek* magazine wrote, "No one came to her aid. No one called police. Some men even cheered. . . ."[2] Again, not one in that tavern crowd would help or even call for help.

Some would say that hate is the opposite of love. It is not. Apathy is. For love is reaching out to others, seeking involvement in their lives, wanting to touch and help others, acting with their best interests in mind. Love is taking the risk of fully engaging oneself in life. Apathy is exactly the opposite. It is withdrawal from the lives of others, uncaring indifference, refusal to act or to risk love in an uncertain world.

Joe Delaney, a runningback for the Kansas City Chiefs football team, drowned recently while trying to save a young girl who had gone in over her head. He knew he could not swim. But he also knew that he could not stand by and watch a young girl drown without trying to save her. This is love breaking through the ice of our apathetic world.

As Christians, we must be willing to take the risk of love. We need to decide ahead of time what we will do if we find ourselves in a position that calls for a loving response. As ambassadors for Christ in our day, we should be prepared to courageously stand in this gap for Christ. The world lives in fear. It is the common and accepted thing today for people not to get involved. But love will take a stand against this trend. Christians who are willing to take the risk of loving action will have an impact and honor Christ in our day.

Once, while my family was living in Minnesota, I was returning home late from a fishing trip. It was pouring down rain. I drove past a man who was drenched and standing on the shoulder of the freeway with his hand out. I went on for another mile or so, then decided to go back and pick him up.

He tossed his pack through the tailgate and stepped in. He was in his early twenties though he had looked older, standing bearded and bent over in the downpour. He was dirty, ragged, soaked to the skin. He told me his name was Lynn.

He had been traveling for more than a month: from Oregon to Texas and east, up the coast and then back to Chicago. "You have to be careful in the big cities," he explained. "Hitchhikers are beaten and robbed."

As we neared the turnoff that would take me home, it was nearly dark. I asked him how late he would be on the road. He said it didn't pay to try to get a ride after dark. He would get off at the next overpass, climb to the top of the concrete bank and sleep on the ledge beneath the bridge.

My inner prompting was to invite this stranger home for the night, but my fearful self spoke strongly about my responsibility for the safety of my family. Then I told myself that I didn't owe this young man anything. Why should I get more deeply involved? And I felt that I had already been a good Samaritan by going out of my way to give him a lift. Yet, it seemed that God wanted me to take a further step. God gave me the courage to choose to trust him.

Judie was already concerned because I was so late getting home. She was cordial but observably nervous when I introduced Lynn and told her I had invited him to stay the night. She recovered quickly and the tension began to disappear while we ate our evening meal. Afterward, Lynn took a shower (he hadn't had one for twenty-eight days), and we talked for about an hour. Then he went upstairs to the guest room across the hall from our four-year-old daughter.

At breakfast we prayed together. When Lynn asked us why we would do something like this, inviting him home to spend the night, we told him how we had become Christians, and what believing in Jesus meant to us. We were surprised that an open relationship could develop in such a short time. After breakfast we drove Lynn out to the highway and let him off. Then he was gone.

There is no way to measure how an experience like this might affect a person like Lynn. But in a few weeks we got a letter from him. He expressed his thanks and said that he had been telling others he met as he hitchhiked home about these Christian people who had taken him in for the night. He wrote, "They can't believe that there are still people in the world who would do something like that."

Love and Risk
Judie and I considered prayerfully why it was hard for us to extend ourselves in love to this stranger. We saw that fear and apathy played a much larger part in our patterns than we thought. In a world where violent crime is an everyday occurrence, we had subtly become closed in our Christian walk, turned in on ourselves. We decided we had to rethink what it means to trust God with our lives.

God does not call us to pick up every hitchhiker we encounter.

But he may call us to pick up some. Being reasonably careful is quite different from being closed. We decided that God might ask us again to act in other situations which would not guarantee our personal safety. And if he did, we hoped we would be ready. Love always requires some measure of risk. We thought about Lynn telling everyone he met that Christians were the only people on his whole trip who invited him in for a night. By trusting God and extending ourselves to others in our uncertain world, Christ will be lifted up. We will be the aroma of Christ to the world.

Recently I had another opportunity to step into an unusual situation of risk. Judie was away for the weekend. I was driving to church with the kids on Sunday morning when we noticed a car that had pulled off on the right side of a short stretch of highway. As we neared, we saw a man and a woman struggling in the ditch. The man was throwing the young woman around. She would fall and try to get up and he would grab her and throw her down again.

Without thinking, I stopped, got out, went down into the ditch and helped the woman up. The man was so shocked that he did nothing as I escorted the woman back to our van. I remember seeing the four wide-eyed faces of my children pasted against the front windshield, taking the whole thing in. We drove to church. The man followed closely behind.

The woman wanted to call the police. She said her husband was a problem drinker, insanely jealous and abusive to her when he was drunk. I could tell she had been drinking too. I didn't know what to do. When we got to church, I had my family take the woman to my office while I talked with her husband. After he had calmed down, we both went up to talk with his wife.

She was willing to be with him again in the security of the church office, so I left them alone for a while and went to teach my class. After class I returned and took the half-hour before my next Sunday morning duty to help them sort out some things. They both knew that they needed counseling and being in a church brought back strong memories for them of good church experiences in their childhood. They expressed a desire to become active again and to give their children a healthy Christian environment in which to grow. I gave them some names of people they could contact in a church in their own town. They left in pretty good shape, committed to doing something. I phoned the pastor of the church in the town where they lived, and he said he would be in touch with them.

Again, there is no way to measure how much change an experience like this may bring in another's life. But the fact that I would stop and get involved spoke deeply to both of these people, even though the man would much rather have had me stay out of things at first.

You never know when you will be called on to take the risk of love. It may be a life-threatening situation for you and even for your family. Or it may be a lower-risk opportunity like staying to make an accurate eyewitness report after observing an accident, or standing up and appearing as a witness to a crime. Wherever Christians see a chance to make a difference in the world by choosing involvement, they should choose it.

As Jesus said the great commandment is to love God and to love our neighbors as ourselves. When a lawyer asked him who his neighbor was, Jesus told the story of the good Samaritan. Here is the paradigm for the risk of love. Christians will be good Samaritans. We will take the time to involve ourselves, even at great personal cost and risk, in the lives of our neighbors.

In our day people will say, Why would he do that? Why would he take that risk? And the answer can be, Because he loved. "Greater love has no one than this," Jesus said, "that he lay down his life for his friends" (Jn 15:13). If we are serious about our Christian commitment, we will be serious about following the example of costly love in the life and death of Christ for us.

Jesus also said, "By this all men will know that you are my disciples, if you love one another" (Jn 13:35). The failure to be obedient in love is ultimately the failure of the Christian to witness the glory of Christ in the church and to the world. We are called to love our neighbors with the costly love of Christ. When we do, we stand out against the prevalent apathy of our contemporary world.

This is a great opportunity for Christians to be the aroma of Christ in the world today.

For Individuals or Groups

1. Do you think that apathy rather than hate is the true opposite of love? Explain.

2. In what ways do you see the church and individual Christians today becoming apathetic?

What can be done about this?

3. On page 28, the author says, "Being reasonably careful is quite different from being closed." How would you explain the difference?

4. Do you believe God may call you and other Christians to act in situations that are life-threatening? If so, how do you feel about that?

5. How can individual Christians and the corporate church become better prepared and more willing to risk acting responsibly for Christ in our day?

3
Building Bridges in Our Neighborhoods

W e chose our neighborhood carefully. We bought our home on a cul-de-sac of predominantly young families. It was important for us to have that traditional family feel—married couples with young children, starting their lives together. And we wanted community, shared lives, a network of caring.

The first thing we noticed when we moved in, though, was that people did not seem as eager to meet us as we were to meet them. Our moving day was ignored by our neighbors. Later we found out why. Moving in and out was common here. Every few months the neighborhood would experience another move. So why should anyone make a big thing out of it?

It appeared that we had chosen a middle-income neighborhood

which was a good place to buy in, build some equity and move up. So it made sense that people were cool toward us. Why spend time getting to know a family if they were just going to move out of your life a year later?

We tried to be friendly. We prayed for our neighbors and asked God to give us just one good relationship to build on. For the first few years, it didn't happen. Instead, we watched the neighborhood collapse around us. We couldn't believe our eyes.

We lost seven traditional families in a little over three years. We now found ourselves living on a block with three divorced ladies trying to make a go of it with their children, a thoroughly modern young couple dedicated to a two-career-and-no-children lifestyle, a male homosexual couple, a house full of college kids and a most unusual family with five teen-age boys, each with his own pickup truck. They lived in the two-bedroom ranch across the street.

One family, besides ours, stayed on the block. At least this man would talk with me. But it seemed that every time we did talk, at some point in the conversation he would hint that the neighborhood was a pretty decent place until about the time we moved in. We didn't do very well with the family with the teen-age boys either. Judie took them a pitcher of lemonade and some glasses on their moving day. We never got the pitcher or the glasses back, and when we mentioned it to the man, he said he couldn't remember us bringing anything over. And that was the end of the conversation.

We started thinking about moving ourselves. Our own children were growing and we were cramped for space. It was either move or add on. We prayed about this for some time. Finally we decided to build an addition and stay in the neighborhood. Judie and I have always believed in the providential nature of some circumstances, and we couldn't help but think that God might have placed us in this particular neighborhood for a reason.

As the new room went up on top of the garage, the whole neighborhood took notice. The addition was like a symbol of something new and different for our block. A family was choosing to stay, to sink their roots down deeper. It had a tremendous impact. Many in the neighborhood seemed suddenly to trust us more. Choosing to stay and build was a visible statement of our commitment to them and to the neighborhood.

Then, after nearly four years, we began to see some things opening up. The thoroughly modern couple next door came to dinner at our house. They told us when they left that they had never had so much fun with children before. They began inviting our kids into their home and into their yard to jump on the trampoline. Within a year, she was pregnant, and they made it clear to us that it was being around our kids that helped them make a decision to expand their family.

After their little girl was born, the woman went back to work. Judie sat with the little girl during the day. It was the beginning of a fine friendship. After inviting them to a Christmas concert at the church, the woman started coming to church regularly. She is still struggling with the question of how Jesus Christ relates to her life. We're certain that something good will come from her honest questioning.

Then a woman down the block who lives alone with her son, contracted a life-threatening illness. Even though we had only talked a few times, she was open to us coming in to help. She especially wanted to know more about the church and its programs for kids. Eventually she went through the new member's class, and her teenager is involved and enjoying the junior-high program. We have grown close.

Neighborhoods provide excellent opportunities for Christians to be ambassadors for Christ. I'm sure there are many neighborhoods where the changes I have described have not occurred as rapidly, and things are more open and more stable. But I'm also certain that everyone faces apathy to some degree, whether in a traditional neighborhood or an apartment or condominium complex.

I have thought too about the mix of people and families on our block. It is simply not as easy as it once was to relate to others. You don't know what to expect when you knock on someone's door today. Most of the time you can't be positive that the couple living there are married or, if they are married, whether this is the first time. Kids in families have different last names. More than any other time in our history, neighborhoods have become a mix of different nationalities, cultures and unusual modern lifestyles. This is why in most neighborhoods communication has to be worked at. And so people choose to live in isolation from their neighbors rather than to make the risky effort to break through the barriers. While it is understandable, few in our neighborhoods are gutsy enough to stick their necks out.

But Christians have a reason to reach out in love. We have a model in Jesus who attacked all barriers to relationship—whether class, cultural or national. He spent time with religious leaders in the community, and he ate with prostitutes and tax collectors. And because he did, these people were changed.

We are ambassadors for Christ, his representatives on temporary assignment in our neighborhoods. What are some of the things we can do to allow God to make his appeal through us?

The Art of Small Talk
We should make small talk our major ministry in our neighborhoods. We need to be willing to give ourselves to people where they are, in the ordinary, everyday task of living. Small talk is the natural language of the reality of everyday lives. We should become proficient in it. We can learn to enjoy those brief encounters that we are privileged to share with our neighbors.

We should be careful not to be condescending. Nor should we always have to steer the conversation to some prescribed salvation pitch. We are not trying to make something happen but trying to be a part of what is happening, without controlling or manipulating relationships. Your neighbors ought to be able to relax with you, to learn that they can trust you, that you really are interested in them as people first, and that you don't just see them as another potential notch on your Bible binding.

I've observed an interesting phenomenon. Often when I see one of my neighbors, perhaps getting the mail or doing some yard work, I'll go over and strike up a conversation. In a minute or two someone else will come over and join in. Pretty soon we will have several people there chatting and getting to know one another better. I believe that most people want relationship and community with their neighbors but are not sure how to go about it. When they see it happening, they eagerly join in. As Christians in our neighborhoods, we can reach out to others and model friendship behavior by being good listeners, by making it easy for people to talk with us, and by making time for neighbors.

Most of your neighbors' lives will not be lived in crisis but in the ordinary. Learning the art of small talk will help us to become a significant part of the ordinary lives of those around us. I find that if we can become a significant part of their ordinary lives, when crisis comes, we will be invited in there too.

It was during normal small talk that the woman down the block let us know about the extent of her illness. She let us in because we had taken the time earlier to get to know her. We had successfully communicated the true fact that she meant something to us as a person.

Recently a younger couple experienced a sudden layoff from work. This was another couple we had talked with on several occasions and with whom we had shared an evening. When I found out about the layoff, I felt comfortable asking about their finances, and they felt comfortable being honest. We were able to arrange a gift from our church deacons' fund to help them when their rent was due, and within a month he found work through an interview with a plant manager who was a member of our church. Their family started coming to church regularly and we enjoyed good fellowship with them until they made a job-related transfer.

It is easy to make small talk. Careers and kids are good topics. Hobbies, sports, family activities, current events, positive aspects of the neighborhood, property items (cars, boats, pets, gardens, houses, furniture, appliances and so on), home improvement projects, books, films, eating places nearby, where they lived before coming here and even religious topics are all great discussion starters. The most important element is that you are willing to take the time to be with neighbors. Communicate to them that there is nothing more important for you to do with your time than to talk with them and find out more about them.

Make opportunities to get to know your neighbors. Be generous about having neighbors in for a meal or over for a barbecue. Each time you invite a family in, say something important to them about wanting to get to know them. You will find that people will often invite you into their homes once they have been to yours. Invite more than one family over to encourage them to get to know each other better. Plan simple meals that make everyone comfortable. This lets the others know that they can have you and others over without making it a costly affair.

Keep your eye open for opportunities to do things together with your neighbors. Again, it may be a shared interest you have in sports or a hobby or certain family outings, building or crafts. Inviting a neighbor to go fishing or hiking could open up a lasting and significant relationship.

Think of other ways you might be able to open relationships with your neighbors. If you have a videotape machine, you might have a monthly family movie in your home and invite families in. I've known couples who have had a good response to parenting discussions they've held in their homes. And, of course, if the opportunity presents itself, the neighborhood Bible study is still the most effective way to bring truth into the lives of your neighbors.

Judie and I both try to meet new neighbors quickly. We usually take something in on moving day, a pitcher of iced tea or a casserole for their evening meal. We also try to have new neighbors over quickly. It seems like the longer you wait to make that initial contact, the tougher it becomes. Walls begin to grow up that are hard to break through. When you meet new neighbors, work hard at getting their names and using them correctly each time you see them. Remembering names is an important way to say you are personally interested in your new neighbors.

It all comes back to the art of small talk. This is usually the way in. If you haven't formed some basis for relationship by being present and available in the ordinary day-to-day of being a neighbor, you generally will not be let in at a deeper level. And it is during these times of sharing the everyday aspects of life that you will hear needs expressed which open doors for you to demonstrate the practical love of Christ.

Ministering Practical Love

A second important aspect to being the aroma of Christ to our neighbors is taking advantage of every opportunity to care for them in practical, down-to-earth ways.

A young woman whom I recently counseled told me that she grew up in a neighborhood with several Christian families. These Christian neighbors have had a constant and pervasive loving influence on that neighborhood for as long as she can remember.

She recalls many mornings when it snowed during the night and her family got up to find their walk and drive already shoveled. No one would ever know for sure which Christian family had done it. At other times they would go away for vacations and come home to find that their lawn had been watered and mowed and their vegetable and flower garden weeded while they were away. This kind of practical, second-mile, loving action had a tremendous effect on this young girl. She said it was a major reason why she always knew that Christianity was true.

Keeping our eyes open for little ways we can help will have the same effect. Someone is always doing something that requires an extra set of hands. We must, however, be sensitive, not pushing ourselves on others. Most of your neighbors enjoy working on their own home projects and would, for most things, prefer to work alone. You wouldn't, for instance, run over to your neighbor and ask him if you could push his mower for him every other time around the yard. This would only make you a nuisance. But watch for opportunities to help when your help is really needed.

That might mean emergency babysitting, helping to carry in a heavy appliance, preparing meals when a neighbor is sick, or offering advice in an area of expertise such as auto mechanics or electrical work. These are all ways we can love our neighbors with sensitive and practical love.

Pets and Kids

Loving your neighbors' kids and pets can be an open door into relationship. Are you willing to take care of your neighbors' pets while they are away? This is usually a fairly easy thing to do that means a great deal to the family on vacation.

Have you considered making it a fairly regular practice to invite one of the neighbor kids along when you go for ice cream, or to the pool, or fishing, or to some sporting event? You need times to be with your own family alone. But there are often times when including someone else could help to build the relational network in your neighborhoods. Your kids should feel free to ask friends along to Sunday school. This is another way that families can eventually come into contact with church life and the love of Christ.

My own three boys love to play football. We seldom play a game anymore without having a number of the neighbor kids join in. I find that this is a good time to influence kids in the aspect of good sportsmanship and team play. We have good competition which is fun and fair, and we let everyone play. We even moved our games from the back to the front to be more accessible to the neighbors.

Earlier I mentioned Judie's choice to sit with our young neighbor's new daughter. Judie's love for the little girl really came through. The mother was touched by the reality of Judie's love for a child not her own. The little girl enjoyed our boys and they enjoyed her. It opened the way for many hours of visiting that led to the building of a meaningful friendship between our families.

Staying Put
As I mentioned before, deciding to build an addition rather than move out had a tremendous impact on our relationships with our neighbors.

All of us as Christians should consider carefully our moves out of neighborhoods. It takes a great deal of time for relationships to grow and for love to make its way into people's hearts. If we give our neighborhoods time and if we are patient, we will see good things happen. By choosing to stay put, we can swim against the current of upward mobility and say something important about our commitment to the people who live around us.

When Judie and I considered our move, nothing major had begun to happen for us in our neighborhood. But there were some good signs. We decided that if we moved it would be like a gardener preparing the soil, fertilizing, tilling, smoothing, planting the seed and nurturing it, watering the plants, cultivating, and then abandoning the garden to weeds just before harvesting the crop. It didn't make sense to us.

So we chose to stay. And building our addition made a difference on our block. We were no longer seen as just another family buying in for a short time to build the necessary equity so we could move to a better neighborhood. It may take time for fruit to come from your neighborhood ministry, but you realize later that every bit of effort is worth it.

These are some ways that we can become the aroma of Christ to our neighbors. If we remember the importance of salvation appeal—that we are dedicated to laying down our lives in service to others, sensitive and aware of their personal needs, and engaged in meeting those needs with second-mile living and loving—we will become appealing Christians who will impact our neighborhoods for Christ today.

For Individuals or Groups

1. Describe your neighborhood. What kinds of people live near and around you? Are there built-in barriers to relationship and communication? What are they? How might you overcome them?

2. List as many neighborhood outreach skills as you can recall from reading this chapter.

3. Which of the outreach skills mentioned in this chapter would be most effective in helping to build bridges and community in your neighborhood?

4. How can the principles in this chapter be applied to outreach in the other neighborhoods in our lives—at school, on the job, with our relatives, in other relational neighborhoods?

5. How might the shy person begin to gain skill and confidence in making small talk with strangers?

6. What one idea from this chapter can you put into practice this week?

4
The Transparent Marriage

I*t is no secret that the past two decades have brought a* devastating and chaotic decline in the practice of traditional family life.

Broken families are edging toward becoming the norm today rather than the exception. Over fifty per cent of all marriages now end in divorce.[1] This places the rate of American divorces at about twenty-three thousand each week, and the number is still on the rise.

This pervasive trend has infected our attitudes toward marriage and family. A recent Associated Press poll asked Americans whether they thought "most couples getting married today expect to remain married for the rest of their lives." A sixty per cent majority said no.[2]

When the expectations of our population regarding the stability of family life are so low, it is no wonder the brokenness quotient continues to grow.

In a newspaper article on the topic, "Is there life after divorce?" a young woman wrote these tragic and revealing words: "There's no place in my life for fairy tales anymore. Most of us search for the one and only, the perfect love of our lives. There is no one and only, in my opinion. There is, however, the best possible companion available at the best possible time."[3]

Our young people today who grow up in this tragic environment experience firsthand the pain that these abstract statistics cannot begin to describe. They live in these trends, and they have begun to give up hope and trust in committed, long-term relationships. Without the faintest notion of how beautiful and fulfilling a marriage under God can be, these young people drift into and out of relationships with "the best possible companion available at the best possible time." The shallow words of Steven Stills's hit song have become a slogan for the relational expectations of our times, "If you can't be with the one you love, love the one you're with."

Over half of our young people now believe it is not wrong for couples to live together outside of marriage. But a casual attitude toward commitment only increases the dissatisfaction and pain of life. Living together is no way to measure what a completely loyal relationship might bring. When the first real crunch comes, the sign always goes up in the playhouse window, "Waterbed for sale. Young couple drifting apart."

Shifting Trends
A number of factors have had a destructive effect on traditional thinking about marriage and family. The sexual revolution of the sixties and seventies led to experimentation that was harmful to the higher notion of being committed sexually to one person for life. Sex has become increasingly available outside the marriage relation-

ship. Adultery is easy today and to some extent even expected. It is no wonder that so many find it difficult to achieve the committed focus that is necessary for a successful and growing marriage relationship.

There has also been a shift today in the thinking about what brings satisfaction and happiness in life. Our modern culture preaches that happiness is the result of fulfilling one's own desires. This is, of course, a trap. Our own desires are often contradictory. To fulfill one desire usually means we have to deny another at the same time. And when we satisfy some desire we have, there is only another hunger there to take its place. This self-fulfillment strategy brings frustration rather than contentment. But the idea has captured American minds and it too runs in opposition to the responsible and committed demands of love.

Also, until recently, an ever-expanding economy played into the quest for self-fulfillment, creating the apparent freedom to have more, travel more, work less. During this kind of onward and upward economic growth, the need for families to hang together through thick and thin has been less evident. For many, family life is viewed as nothing more than an unnecessary burden standing in the way of individual freedom, self-fulfillment and, therefore, happiness.

Americans too have grown impatient with anything which does not immediately add to the satisfaction quotient of their personal lives. Many of the older ideas such as *nothing good is ever achieved without the pain of hard work* or that *good things (including good relationships) do not happen overnight* or that *the best things in life are worth waiting for* have been called into question. The drive for immediate sensual satisfaction has been at the core of the behavior of our generation for years. When the immediate rewards in a new marriage wear thin (usually shortly after the honeymoon), many today are not prepared to take the more important steps toward deeper commitment. They look instead for other satisfactions that are often focused on self and are ultimately destructive to the marriage relationship.

These are just a few of the cultural shifts that have created the atmosphere in which selfish choices can be made more easily. Coupled with the truth that real marriages and deep relating require an immense amount of hard work and constant, loving attention, it is no wonder that so many have tried to find happiness in places where society promised it could be had with little personal cost or effort.

There is a positive side to all of this. Recent statistics have begun to show that there may be a pendulum swing toward a new ethic of commitment in our country. This is coupled with a newly stated desire by an increasing number of Americans for deeper and long-lasting relationships. In 1973, only thirty-two per cent of all Americans suggested that human community and relationship were a high priority. These statistics are in line with what we would expect to find at the height of our age of self-fulfillment. But surprisingly, by the early eighties, the same survey was repeated and produced a response of forty-seven per cent who stated that human relationships were a high priority. This is a tremendous increase in such a short time.[4]

Perhaps the self-fulfillment fantasy is running its course. The cover of a recent *Esquire* magazine pictures a young, attractive, healthy-looking, casually dressed woman. She gives us a lonely look as she says, "I have a good job and a condo on the beach. I run four miles a day and play tennis twice a week. I'm in perfect health, and my roller skates cost $100. I guess you could say I'm . . . unhappy." Instead of fruitful living, self-fulfillment has brought sour grapes. And now, when so many self-proclaimed societal prophets are still predicting the total demise of the traditional family, a new poll among marrieds and singles alike shows that ninety-six per cent declare themselves dedicated to the ideal of two people sharing a life and home together.[5]

Models of Hope

This dramatic growth in the felt need for deep and lasting relationships creates a new open door for Christians today. We have something to say to those who desire—but do not know how to achieve—lasting, growing relationships. We know it is possible to live out commitment in our day. And we know that loving relationships which draw their strength from God bring the fruit of happiness, joy and mutual caring that the disillusioned in our day desire. Our marriages can model the reality of relationships that stand in opposition to the hopeless attitudes of so many.

Having a good marriage and raising an effective family today is not easy, but it is possible with the sustaining grace of God who wants his design for human community to be successful. Broken relationships have caused great pain in the world. Christians can work to recreate an atmosphere of hope—not a mere belief in fairy tales but hope in the power of committed love to make a marriage relationship work and grow and become increasingly exciting and throughout a couple's married life. We will accomplish this best by having good marriages that work, and by dedicating ourselves to having transparent relationships which others can observe.

Some of the simplest things in our marriages will often communicate the presence of Christ's love to others. The fact that your husband or wife is obviously your best friend, that you like spending time with each other, that you talk and walk together, that you simply enjoy being with each other, is a witness to a broken world that true and committed love is still possible in our times. Your willingness to touch and show affection speaks more loudly than all your wise words on love and marriage. Husbands and wives who laugh together and have fun with each other testify to what can be. Showing your pride in each other's achievements and speaking well of each other in social situations, when others deliver cutting complaints behind the backs of their husbands and wives, will also speak to the radical difference of your love. And telling the story of how your marriage gets better and better as you grow through the years together will demonstrate that the power of Christ is alive in your relationship.

Being Real

Judie and I have learned, though, that the most powerful witness to Jesus in this area is not an ideal, picture-perfect marriage, but a real marriage that struggles, grows and improves through the forgiveness and grace of God in Christ. Our neighbors are less interested in observing an exterior of idealistic perfection than they are in seeing how the real marriage experiment can work in the face of true difficulties that come into normal family life. The marriage experiment that works today, that is able to manage well the stresses that come to married life through the uncertainties of this modern world, declares the existence of the love and power of Christ.

Our best witness is a truly transparent marriage. Those around us need to see that we face the same struggles they face. They need to see that we make mistakes and that our kids make mistakes, that we are on the whole living in the same world they are. The difference though will come as they observe the reality of Jesus' love operating in our marriages. It is in the miracle of seeing real life lived and genuine experiences of pain resolved that our neighbors will be drawn to the life-changing love of Jesus Christ.

Once, when our four children were small, they teamed up one summer day to see how much damage they could cause in our back yard in one morning. I won't go into the horrible details. The result was that after the third or fourth incredible misbehavior, Judie came storming out of the house determined to make a final and lasting impression. The whole neighborhood heard what was going on.

Judie was terribly upset with herself for losing her cool. But later that afternoon a most surprising thing happened. Our neighbor over the back fence came over to talk. She told Judie that what had happened in the morning gave her more hope for the success of her own family. She reasoned this way. She had observed our family life and saw that it was successful. She saw Judie as a perfect parent, always in control, always doing the right things at the right times. She knew herself and knew she was not a perfect parent. She had begun to lose hope for her family. But what she had observed earlier that day in our back yard said to her that it might be possible to have a good and loving family even if everybody is not perfect all the time. She learned that forgiveness operates in a Christian family and that grace covers the human sin of failure.

The situation created an opening for Judie to talk about what it means for our family to be living under the grace of God. Judie's vulnerability was the open door to talking with our neighbor about Christ. Judie's previous apparent perfection as a parent had been a barrier to communication between them.

Sometimes Christians feel that they must keep up the perfect appearance in order to witness significantly for Christ. Often the opposite is true. Letting people see that Jesus makes a difference in the real life situations of our pain and need is the most powerful witness of all.

Being Transparent

We do not have to be afraid to let people see God at work in our families. Our neighbors should know that forgiveness lives in our houses. But the reality of forgiveness suggests the need for reconciliation. We forgive because something has gone wrong. If we are transparent, they will see that this is so. And our neighbors should observe our dependence on God in prayer, our trusting attitude.

We turn to God with greatest intensity when we are in the midst of family struggle or pain. If we are transparent, our neighbors will see the dependence on God, but they will also see the struggles and pain. Jesus' love makes a difference in real life. Our best witness is always to live transparently and let others observe Christ's love healing our relationships, calling us to live in forgiveness, and making it possible for us to live thankfully and joyfully in the real world.

Think of the following witness of transparent love observed, marked and recorded by Richard Selzer, a surgeon:

I stand by the bed where a young woman lies, her face post-operative, her mouth twisted in palsy, clownish. A tiny twig of the facial nerve, the one to the muscles of her mouth, has been severed. She will be thus from now on. The surgeon had followed with religious fervor the curve of her flesh; I promise you that. Nevertheless, to remove the tumor in her cheek, I had cut the little nerve.

Her young husband is in the room. He stands on the opposite side of the bed, and together they seem to dwell in the evening lamplight, isolated from me, private. Who are they, I ask myself, he and this wry-mouth I have made, who gaze at and touch each other so generously, greedily? The young woman speaks.

"Will my mouth always be like this?" she asks.

"Yes," I say, "it will. It is because the nerve was cut."

She nods, and is silent. But the young man smiles.

"I like it," he says. "It is kind of cute."

All at once I *know* who he is. I understand, and I lower my gaze. One is not bold in an encounter with a god. Unmindful, he bends to kiss her crooked mouth, and I, so close, can see how he twists his own lips to accommodate to hers, to show her that their kiss still works. I remember that the gods appeared in ancient Greece as mortals, and I hold my breath and let the wonder in.[6]

The pain of life comes to each of us in time. The world claims we can escape pain, sickness, aging and death. But we can't. And sooner or later everyone realizes that if happiness requires living a pain-free life the project of happy living is doomed to failure. True happiness is not escaping pain, but learning to live resourcefully and joyously in the midst of pain. It seems that Jesus is not as concerned with whether we have a particular success or failure in life as he is with how we meet our successes and failures.

I asked a retired friend, whose wife was stricken early in their marriage with debilitating meningitis, to tell me what has sustained them through the years. He said that they married for better or for worse, to live together rich or poor, in sickness or in health. He explained that many never experience, as they had, the blessed opportunity to live out their marriage vows.

They saw her illness as an opportunity to live commitment to the limit, and to explore the demands and blessings of love more deeply than is normally possible. Their love for one another and the strength and quality of their character is evident. This kind of transparent love observed in the context of the real world stands as a testimony to the reality that God is at work, and that the mystery of life-changing love is still present and available through Christ today for those who hunger for the deeper dimensions of life.

For Individuals or Groups

1. The author contends that trying to find happiness by fulfilling all of one's own desires is a trap. Do you agree or disagree? Why?

2. What factors or changes in our society have contributed to the breakdown of marriage and family?

3. What is your reaction to the statement, "The most powerful witness to Jesus in this area is not an ideal, picture-perfect marriage, but a real marriage that struggles, grows and improves through the forgiveness and grace of God in Christ" (p. 46)? How, if at all, have you seen this to be true?

4. On page 48, Eisenman writes, "True happiness is not escaping pain, but learning to live resourcefully and joyously in the midst of pain." Is this idealistic or realistic? Explain.

In what situations, if any, have you observed this to be true?

5. Express in your own words what you think it means to have a transparent marriage.

6. What fears do we have that keep us from being more transparent and vulnerable in our marriage relationship?

How might we overcome these fears?

5

The Witness of Christian Children

Nothing convinces us more thoroughly of the values vacuum and moral indecisiveness of our times than the behavior of children raised by today's confused parents.

I don't think there has ever been a time when I've witnessed so much selfishness, meanness, rudeness and disobedience in children. And I've never seen as much disrespectful arguing with parents and talking back. A casual walk through the supermarket today will produce numerous examples of children out of control. They scream and kick and wail until mom or dad gives in and buys the candy bar or gum or whatever it is they want, positively reinforcing their temper tantrums. Parents seem helpless and totally lost.

Last winter in our kindergarten Sunday school, kids were lining up to move from one room to another. I saw a five-year-old boy wind up and whip another boy ahead of him across the face with his jacket, cutting the boy's cheek with his zipper. The mother was standing right there, observing her son's vicious behavior. She turned and said sweetly to some of the rest of the parents, "Oh, boys will be boys."

Recovering a Lost Vision

We seem to have lost a vision for our children. We have so thoroughly given in to the secular drift in child rearing and have so willingly accepted the diminished product of our efforts, that we no longer believe that our children could really be more.

When Judie and I were new Christians in a small church in Wisconsin, one of the elders invited us over after the Sunday evening service for tea. His youngest boy rode with us to show us the way. We have never forgotten the quality of the conversation we had with this young man who talked about his faith in Christ and what a difference being Christian had made to him and to his whole family. We were astounded by his sincerity and maturity. He told us how happy he was for us and said we had many wonderful things ahead of us because we now had a relationship with Jesus. He was a powerful witness to us of how Christ can enrich a family and give even young children the mark of his secure love.

A major concern we have as Christian parents is the issue of authority. This is really the central issue in Christianity. Will we respond to proper authority, or will we rebel? Children need to learn to submit themselves to proper authority, and if we fail to teach this, we fail in our task of preparing our children for effective Christian living.

God gives us the model for parenting in Hebrews 12:4-13. Verse 6 says, ". . . the Lord disciplines those he loves." Verse 11 helps us understand the role of discipline and gives us a promise. "No discipline seems pleasant at the time, but painful. Later on, however, it produces a harvest of righteousness and peace for those who have been trained by it." The passage teaches that truly loving parenting will be a combination of unconditional love and affirmation accompanied with decisive, no-nonsense discipline when it is called for.

We need to have a vision for our children so that we can help them become all that they can be for Christ. As parents, we decide on the basis of the biblical material what qualities we believe God would want to see developed in our children. Then we work diligently as partners in cooperation with the Holy Spirit to encourage the maturing of our children toward those biblical goals.

We will find that there are some things that should be true for the behavior of Christian children in general. We would expect, for instance, to observe a growing interest in the things of God, as the child includes God in thoughts, talk and play. Children should also be developing a giving attitude that recognizes the importance of unselfish sharing. Learning how and when to say, "I'm sorry," is a difficult but essential biblical life principle. Children should grow in their ability to empathize and sympathize with others, developing the skills needed to encourage rather than criticize. As a general principle, Christian children should show an increasing willingness to act in accordance with their developing conscience under parenting that is guided by the Spirit and the values inherent in the law of God.

More important than anything else, though, is that our children demonstrate a developing confidence and self-esteem that develops as they grasp and internalize the fact that God loves them unconditionally, and we do too. Parents teach this kind of complete and unconditional love when they allow their children the freedom to fail, forgive their kids quickly and easily, and praise good efforts over a perfectly finished product. Children will in this context feel free to reach for new experiences, to risk failure. They will not have to deal with the burden of trying to gain parental love and acceptance by behaving perfectly or achieving a perfect result with every project. When we make the mistake of praising our children when their work is well done, and ignoring or ridiculing them when it is not, we give them the strong message that our love for them depends on their achievement. The joy and happiness our children feel in regard to themselves and their lives will be a sign to us that they have begun to understand and appropriate the most basic reality in the Christian faith, the grace of God's unconditional love.

There should also be individual goals for different children in a family because God has given each child important personal distinctives. Here parents should be aware of individual gifts and how to encourage the growth of these special qualities. Each child will also have individual problem areas that need to be addressed. It is perhaps an understatement to say that nurturing and training our children is a difficult and demanding full-time job that requires sustained effort, much prayer, and energetic cooperation and communication between parents.

All of the behaviors mentioned above are learned best if they are modeled by the parents in a home atmosphere of loving encouragement and proper control. Parents set the goals for bringing their children up and helping them to learn the significant attitudes and behaviors that mark them as children of God. Parents are charged with this duty and should take control (Eph 6:4). It is wrong to let our children dictate to us a lower standard of behavior than we believe God is calling them to.

Learning from Experience

Judie and I adopted our first child, a darling baby girl. In a short time we nearly ruined her through poor parenting. By positively reinforcing her negative behaviors it did not take long for us to make a monster out of one of the sweetest natural personalities God has ever brought into this world. Jana screamed and cried and threw temper tantrums. She would not play alone. She would not sleep through the night. We were confused and frustrated.

Out of desperation we sought the help of more experienced Christian couples whose children were well behaved. At first we thought we had just been unlucky and had been given a bad kid, stubborn and strong-willed. But little by little we learned from others that we were making significant mistakes in parenting that contributed to Jana's behavior. We saw that our major problem was that we were constantly rewarding Jana's bad behavior. We learned that when you positively reinforce any behavior in your child, you can expect that behavior to grow in intensity and to be repeated. When we quit rewarding Jana's bad behavior and started positively reinforcing her good behavior, things began to turn around.

Accepting the fact that love must sometimes be tough and learning to set standards were hard for us. But as we gained consistency and followed through on basic principles that had worked for others, the results were amazing. We recommend to any couple planning to have children that they observe carefully the love and discipline that occurs in families where the children exemplify the behaviors we hope for in Christian kids. Do not hesitate to seek the advice of these Christian families.

As Jana developed and grew and became a joy to be around, Judie and I decided it was time to enlarge our family again. This time we wanted to make sure that we were being guided in our parenting by a godly vision. After deep thinking and much prayer about our own parental weaknesses, we decided that with God's help we would try to raise children who respect proper authority, who adults would recognize immediately as being different from the norm in this respect.

We had seen that in families where children were both affirmed and disciplined, the children often developed a wide variety of lovely qualities, and we hoped for these things in our own kids. Children from these families were truly loving and gentle, kind to animals and to smaller children than themselves. These were the boys and girls who unselfishly reached out to unpopular kids on the block and at school, receiving them as friends when no one else would. We saw that there were families in which brothers and sisters loved and appreciated each other and took more pleasure in giving and sharing than in having everything for themselves. We came to believe that these things could be possible for our kids, and that they should be prevalent behaviors of children like ours who grow up in Christian families.

Well-behaved children are, unfortunately, such an unusual phenomenon today that they draw a great deal of attention. They are a tremendous testimony to the fact that something extraordinary is happening in a family. We have had people come up to us in restaurants to comment positively on the behavior of our four small children. These little exchanges with people can often be open doors for the gospel. The beautiful thing is that our children have begun to recognize that their appropriate behavior is a strong witness for Jesus. They've seen the warm and positive responses of people toward them. They are glad to know that God can use them in this way to enter the lives of others.

We recently went with a young family to an amusement park in Denver. They have a boy of five, a girl of three and a young baby. Our twins were just nine at the time and our youngest boy was eight. While parents talked, our boys took their two older kids into the kiddie park to show them a good time. One of our twins spent an hour with their little girl, helping her climb into the boats or cars, strapping her in, waving to her as she came by ringing the bell, then helping her out and taking her by the hand to the next ride. Our other two boys showed their older boy a great time as well. The mother told us the next time we saw her that her kids were so taken by our boys that they invented a new game. Now, instead of playing house, they play Eisenmans.

There are no absolute guarantees in parenting. We know that kids are not going to be perfect, and some will turn away from us no matter how good a job of parenting we do. As Joe Bayly has pointed out, God created two perfect children and placed them in a perfect environment, and they still chose to rebel against him. But knowing this should not deter us from working to achieve everything we can for our kids. They will be happier if they are given a stable home environment in which they can mature as young Christian men and women. And if they are strong kids who will love as they have been loved, they will be a witness to the world that Jesus can make an amazing difference in the development of human personality.

Raising good kids takes constant hard work and attention. But if our children are loving and caring, respectful and obedient, they say something powerful today to their peers and to adults around them of the life-changing reality of the Christian faith.

For Individuals or Groups

1. If parents lose their vision for what children can be in Christ, what are some possible results?

2. How can parents teach and demonstrate to their children that they are loved unconditionally?

3. Develop an argument which supports the idea that disciplining our children is really a significant way to demonstrate our love and care for them.

4. Parents often appear to be blind to the misbehavior of their own children. What reasons can you give for this?

5. Respond to the statement, "God created two perfect children and placed them in a perfect environment, and they still chose to rebel against him." What are the implications of this?

6. What resources are available today to help Christian parents develop the skills for effective parenting?

7. If you are a Christian parent, take the time to pray and think about each of your children.

What are their strengths?

How can you positively reinforce your child's positive personality characteristics?

What is one aspect that needs to change? Develop a plan to help your child gain strength in this area.

Remember to spend most of your time positively reinforcing good behavior. Pray each day for each of your children.

6
New Men for a New Day

After I had lunch with a man to discuss a ministry program we were involved with, we walked out and stood together on the sidewalk. It was obvious to both of us that we had begun to develop a meaningful relationship. I told him how much I appreciated his friendship, and I reached out and gave him a hug.

His reaction surprised me a great deal. He had received me as a friend; that was obvious. But the hug in public was difficult for him. He pulled back, embarrassed.

Our relationship is a good one. It does not really matter to me that my friend is uncomfortable hugging in public. In fact, I wouldn't force a hug on someone if I knew ahead that it would make him uncomfortable. But the incident reveals that there is something tragic that has happened to men in our culture. Men have learned a number of things that now may stand in the way of relating naturally with other men and enjoying the deep joy of expressing and receiving love from friends.

The most important thing to God is relationships. His own chosen pattern for existence is the relationship of Father, Son and Holy Spirit (Gen 1:26). Our salvation means entering into a love relationship with Jesus. We become sons and daughters of God, and brothers and sisters to one another in the body of Christ (Eph 1:5; 2:15-16). God's plan for us is to live in meaningful relationships of love and caring, and this obviously includes making and maintaining loving friendships between men (1 Jn 3:11-15).

Most men today hunger for meaningful relationships with other men, but they do not have the skills or freedom of attitude to achieve what they really want and need most. They have been taught among other things that it is unmanly to show emotion. The idea of one man telling another man that he loves him is so contrary to our society's norms for male behavior that to do so in public can be social suicide.

Also, aside from contact sports, men almost never touch one another. Touching—according to the shallow thinking of our culture—has come to automatically imply sexual interest. It is no wonder my friend was uncomfortable with my public expression of gladness for our friendship.

Men today often lack relational skills as well. They have been boxed into a macho image so long that they have never had the opportunity to develop and practice the skills necessary to relate well to others. I have observed how men can meet together daily in a work situation for years while their conversation never moves beyond the shallowest level of jokes, politics and sports. Men do not know how to listen sensitively, to draw others into more meaningful dialog, or to be vulnerable and open with other men.

Another barrier for most men is the intense competitive spirit that they have been taught from an early age. Love means seeking the best for another person, while our modern form of competition says instead, "Take advantage of every weakness to get to the top," and, "Winning is the only important thing." The belief that nice guys finish last is widespread.

Men also have an aversion to asking for help. Any revealed need might be interpreted as a weakness. What a terrible burden rests on the shoulders of men.

Being a Good Friend to Other Men

A quick reading of 1 Samuel 18:1-4 and chapter 20 reveals the biblical contrast to today's cultural norms in the area of men relating to other men.

The friendship of David and Jonathan is rich and meaningful. It can act as a model for us as we try to move our thinking and behavior in the biblical direction.

The passage begins by saying that David and Jonathan loved each other (18:1). They made a covenant together and promised faithfulness in their friendship (18:3). This shows that their friendship was not a casual thing, but a significant relationship that they recognized and chose to promote. We should not be afraid to let our friends know how much we appreciate our growing friendships. Nor should we resist friendship even though it requires a commitment of time and energy.

Friends trust one another (20:1). David needed an honest answer from Jonathan about why Saul was angry with David. Friends are willing to be open and honest with each other because they believe that what they share will be kept in confidence.

Friends are available to one another (20:4). Jonathan said, "Whatever you want me to do, I'll do for you." This is a statement of total availability of person, time and resources for his friend.

A friend is also kind (20:8). This was David's request from his friend. Kindness suggests empathy, the important quality of hurting with your friends when they hurt. And kindness presupposes the ability to listen sensitively to others, gently encouraging them.

Truthfulness and faithfulness are also important qualities in good relationships (20:9-13 and 32-33). Jonathan promised to tell David as soon as he had any inkling that Saul wanted to harm David. And he did. This also shows how candor is necessary to a true friendship. Talking behind another's back, gossiping and lying are prohibited.

Quality friendships also require vulnerability (20:41). Jonathan and David wept openly before each other and kissed each other in a sorrowful farewell. This portion of Scripture may be very difficult for modern men to read. The open showing of emotions and physical expressions of affection between men are not common today. But reading this material on friendship between men shows us how much we have lost. This is one of the truly beautiful passages recorded in Scripture of the love between good friends.

Christian men ought to lead the way in resisting the pressure to conform to the uptight macho image thrust on them by society. David and Jonathan were great men. David as a boy killed the giant Goliath. He was Israel's greatest king. And Jonathan was one of the great military leaders in Old Testament times. But these men were not afraid or ashamed to openly show their affection to one another and to weep together because their deep love and friendship was threatened by Jonathan's own insane father.

Christian men should take every opportunity to learn the skills for effective relating with other men today. My experience is that men everywhere are hungering for relationships that are meaningful, but they don't know how to achieve what they desire most.

This is where Christian men come in. We can learn to listen more sensitively to the needs of others. Being a person who can be trusted will open doors for relationship with other men. And a man who is willing to take the time to meet the practical needs of others will stand out as someone who is positively different. Loving Christian men can have a great impact for Christ in the world of men today.

What might happen if every Christian man reading this book would take the time to be a friend with just one neighbor or one acquaintance at work who appears to need a friend? If you stop for a moment to think about it, you will have no difficulty identifying some man in your circle who needs a friend. If each of us would take the brief amount of time required to phone, have lunch or go fishing with someone like this who needs a friend, we could have a tremendous impact in this area for Christ.

As I'm writing this, I'm thinking about the men's service club of which I am a member. What could happen in our service club if every Christian man there would take the time to concentrate on building a friendship with one other man in the club? It doesn't take that much time or energy to focus on one person and give him the attention of a good friend. By taking this small individual step, we could create thousands of open doors across this country for Jesus to become a part of men's lives.

An attorney friend of mine has had this kind of personal, one-on-one ministry for years. He takes the time to focus on one man at a time who seems to need a friend. He meets with this one individual in an open-ended way, praying that God will open doors for a spiritual connection beyond the human relationship. This friend of mine has also had a small-group Bible study one morning a week for years. Many of his one-on-one friends eventually enter that Bible study and through its ministry have made commitments to Christ.

Another friend of mine who is now retired sets aside three mornings a week to meet regularly with men. He spends time with men he has met outside the church and develops relationships in a natural way, giving God a chance to work through the real love and care he expresses to these men in need.

Who could you be a friend to? Is there a man in your neighborhood or at work with whom you have a natural connection? Pray that God will give you a friend to care for and enjoy, and possibly lead into a relationship with the Savior, Jesus Christ.

Relating Effectively with the Opposite Sex

Another way Christian men can witness for Jesus is by relating more effectively with women. Jesus was a leader in his day in recognizing that the negative treatment of men toward women contradicted the requirements of love inherent in the gospel message.

Many attitudes promoted by radical feminists are direct attacks on the central values of the Christian faith. When marriage is demeaned, for instance, or bearing children, Christians have to be opposed. But Christian men ought to be leaders in supporting those aspects of the women's movement that point up true incidents of injustice and unloving, immoral treatment of women. Christian men ought to be known for their support of change in favor of justice for women in our day. This will be a great witness in our times, that Christian men hold women in the highest regard after the loving model of Jesus himself.

A strong case can be made for the theory that men share a deep insecurity about who they are and what value they have in life. Margaret Mead has written, "The central problem of every society is to define appropriate roles for the men."[1] Men do not appear to have a clearly perceived, meaningful life role provided for them.

If this is true, and men are insecure about their identity and their place in life, their response to women will be tainted by this insecurity. A certain sign of insecurity in human personality is the frightened need to dominate others through manipulation and use of power. This appears to be a consistent historical pattern of behavior for men and a common response in our times.

The New Bedford, Mass., rape of a young woman by a number of working-class men in a tavern is understandable in these terms. New Bedford suffers from a tragically high unemployment rate. Large numbers of women are moving into the modern work force, the traditional domain of men. The young woman in the tavern becomes a symbol for that which is most threatening to men. The men react violently out of a need to assert their dominance. The scene is really a tragic statement about male insecurity and the fragile nature of male ego strength.

If a man is secure, he is psychologically able to freely promote the growth and development of others, including members of the opposite sex. A secure man will not be threatened by a specific woman or by women in general. And this kind of secure response, working in partnership with women and promoting them whenever possible, should be the marked style of loving and secure Christian men in our times.

Christian men have their identity rooted in Christ. They are unquestionably important in their work for Christ in the church, the world and in their families. The work they have been called by Christ to accomplish with him has ultimate and eternal value. Christian men should be free from the need to dominate others, keeping them in an inferior place through the use of manipulation and power.

Again, Christian men should be leaders today in supporting change that enhances more positive behavior and attitudes toward women. When Christian men relate to women rightly and help them become all that they can be, Christ will be honored, and Christian men will witness the love and justice of Christ.

But there is still one more important way that Christian men can have a significant impact for Christ. A pastor on our staff recently told the story of a young woman who came to see him. She was a new Christian, interested in learning how she could grow consistently in her new life. When he asked her how she had become a Christian, she told him that the Christian man she had been dating would not go to bed with her, even though she had urged him to do so. She came to understand through the experience that the young man loved Christ and loved her too much to do anything that had the potential of damaging their relationship or demeaning an experience that was a gift from God. She was so amazed and touched by this uncommon behavior that she wanted to know more about

Jesus. It was not long before she chose to devote herself to Christ for life.

There are many other ways that men can demonstrate their Christian difference and have an impact on those around them. Being better friends to other men, working more effectively with and standing for the just causes of women, and paying attention to the biblical demands for appropriate behavior are just a few. One other major area of impact, for instance, is the witness of a good father and a good husband today. I will not develop this topic because much has been written in the past ten years in this area.

All men should pray deeply and think creatively today about whether we are doing all we can to be the aroma of Christ to those at work, to our families and to those we meet in every other area of life. Christian men will be lovingly different if they think about how the biblical material applies to their lives in a practical, everyday manner. And where they are refreshingly different from other men today, they will affect the world for the cause of Christ.

For Individuals or Groups

1. What social barriers noted in this chapter keep men from achieving meaningful relationships with other men?

What are some other hindrances you can think of that the author has not mentioned?

2. What are the key relational skills that will help Christian men to be more sensitive and effective friends?

What are some practical ways these could be put into effect?

3. If Christian men take advantage of opportunities to learn and practice relational skills, what impact might they have on those around them?

4. Think of one person you know with whom you might strike up a relationship that could be fruitful. What could you do to initiate or enhance this friendship?

5. Do you agree or disagree with the statement, "A secure man will not be threatened by a specific woman or by women in general" (p. 63)? Explain.

6. Review what the author says about ways Christian men can support and encourage women today. What are other ways you can think of that a Christian man's behavior can be significantly different in regard to the treatment of women?

7
The Witness of Working Women

A *young Christian woman I know used to be an* extraordinarily pleasant person to be around. She was committed to her work, creative, interesting, skilled and bright. She had all the qualities that should have made her a compelling witness for Jesus Christ in her workplace. She had, though, one flaw. She tended to be shy, and she became obsessed with doing something about it.

In a period of about two years—during which she took every assertiveness training course offered in the area—she became one of the most difficult people that I have ever known. She was on guard at every moment, making certain that no one, especially no man, would get an edge on her. She saw lurking beneath everyone's external behavior a secret agenda aimed at taking advantage of her shyness. The whole world was out to get her. She was now trained and determined to get them first. She became well known on the community grapevine as a stereotypical corporate barracuda. There no longer seemed to be any connection between the basic values that form the foundation for Christian living and her behavior in the workplace. What had gone wrong?

Career women today certainly face one of the toughest assignments a Christian disciple can have. Prejudice still exists. Men still take advantage of women, pressure women sexually, treat women unfairly, tend to promote men even when a qualified woman is in the running for a position and in general harass women as a ploy to keep them off balance in the psychological game of territorial rights.

Even though all these realities and more are part of the everyday work world of most women, Christian women still have to struggle with what it means to be a Christian and live out Christian values in the face of put-downs and persecution. No Christian, man or woman, can ignore the demands of love at the core of the Christian gospel. Obviously, corporate sharks can never warm the hearts and open the minds of those around them to the positive possibilities of the Christian faith.

As a man, I admit readily that the simple fact that I have not faced daily the same kinds of prejudicial pressures women face at work makes me a poor candidate to write on this subject. I have, however, sought the insight and guidance of a number of professional Christian women who courageously face the struggle of trying to do a competitive job at work while attempting to keep Christian values intact, as well as trying to impact those around them with the love of Christ.

I started interviewing women after reading the analysis of a young Christian executive secretary's work situation in a secular office. Rita Peters of Northern Petrochemical in Omaha writes:

For me, it's smoke-filled rooms, gossip in abundance, listening to swearing, and being considered "different" if I stand for my faith. My manager knows I'm involved in a street ministry, and a couple times he has sarcastically asked me, "Well, how many souls did you save this weekend?"

The pressures and temptations are great, and by the end of the week I feel drained.

Working in a secular job can draw Christians toward their own resources and playing corporate games to get ahead. But their real power comes from God. I would like to see church leaders continuously feed the flock with the message that Christ is in us and that He is our hope of glory. Our hope is not in the business world. Our promotions really come from God, not our managers. We need to see His hand in our business relations.

As working people constantly exposed to secular values, we need to be reminded that God is love, real power, and grace.[1] Rita's focus on God and his absolute power and control of her destiny are, it seems, crucial to keeping one's perspective regarding the importance of a strong Christian witness at the workplace.

A friend of mine attended a conference for Christian professional women in Seattle. I asked her to find out from some of the women there how they manage to keep their heads while trying to be a good witness on the job. The women she spoke with had many insightful and helpful comments.

A marketing representative said, "Be warm and personal. Pray about what God wants you to be and do in your job."

A career counselor felt the strongest witness was to "be competent; perform well on the job."

A lawyer at the conference said, "Don't put down people in 'lower' jobs. Don't hide the fact that you're a Christian." (She openly shares about her involvement in a local youth ministry.) She adds, "Work out relationships. Be the person who addresses problems like poor communication between individuals."

The manager for a manufacturing firm had these things to say about witnessing for Christ on the job: "How Christian women handle themselves under stress says a lot. Don't isolate yourself from non-Christians. On the other hand, accept the fact that as a Christian you will at times be set apart. Don't be self-righteous, taking it upon yourself to improve the moral habits of everyone around you. Lean on the Lord." One interesting thing this woman does is to circulate through her department every Friday afternoon to chat personally with her employees and wish them an enjoyable weekend.

My partner in ministry, Gwen Brown, worked for a number of years in administrative positions at the University of Colorado. When we talked about this topic, Gwen shared with me a number of observations which gave me the core of the written material below.

Fairness and Justice at the Workplace

Strong women activists in the workplace can tend to have an overly simplified value structure. The "good" is what's good for the women. The "bad" is what's bad for the women. Nothing else matters. These women often want special privileges in the workplace solely on the basis of their feminine sex. Gwen told me that she was often caught in a blackmail game where a woman colleague would come to make a request but would essentially be saying, "You're a woman. I'm a woman. This fact should be all that's needed for you to grant me what I want." Christian women should make it a priority to work hard to obtain an accurate and honest appraisal of job and personnel problems and be decisive on the basis of factual evidence, rather than acting out of sexual prejudice.

Christian women will be as fair in their appraisal of the motives of others (including men) as they can be. Although prejudice against women is common in the workplace today, it is still possible that a man may be promoted ahead of a woman on the basis of experience, skill and overall competence.

We are not saying that Christian women will never shake things up at the office. When an injustice occurs, a Christian woman will be at the forefront of the debate. But Christian women should be known for their fairness and objectivity at work. In this, their best witness is to maintain an ethical approach, modeling for others the way all men and women are to be treated and promoted.

Strong Feminine Leadership

Another problem Gwen observed was the number of women who bought into the male style of power-play leadership. Later in this book we will talk about how inappropriate it is for men or women to use manipulative techniques. The suggestion here is that Christian women should be more creative in developing leadership styles consistent with Christian values.

We need strong leaders today who have character, who refuse to play the power games, who will be models for young men and women of management styles that respect honesty, fairness, competence, dedication and care for the lives of employees.

I have seen how the power of God can work through one dedicated woman to change the course of a business. This particular woman made the word *integrity* the motto for her own life and relationships. Shortly after she took a management position where she worked, the whole department began talking about and caring about integrity. Now the company has worked the word into its motto for product, personnel and customer service.

A different but related aspect of leadership for women is the general influence Christian women can have on the attitudinal atmosphere of their work environment. In today's workplace, a staff of employees will sometimes give themselves over to a steady diet of gossip, negativity and swearing. In such a setting a kind of hatred rhetoric will commonly develop in which women continually cut others down, especially men. (The men who enter into this kind of behavior often focus their put-downs on women.) This promotes an atmosphere in which negative generalizations or characterizations of others become a focus for constant irritation.

Christian women can have a tremendous impact in a situation like this by being positive and encouraging, and by working to promote the best possible image of others. Christian women will not be known for putting others down. They should especially resist negative comments aimed at men under women, men on the lower rungs of the corporate ladder. And Christian women will not take part in biting and vicious gossip that feeds the negative atmosphere on the job. Instead of making enemies, lying about others and stifling communication between people, Christian women will strive for honesty in relating, will deal with rock-hard facts, and will promote peace and open communication whenever possible.

Sometimes simple Christian practices will have a tremendous influence on the workplace. Most today will not directly face a problem with another employee to try to work it out. They go over the other person's head to complain to upper management. If a Christian decided to handle every problem by meeting face to face with the other person involved, as the Bible suggests (Mt 18:15), she could have a profound effect on the way problems are solved. This practice alone could build and enhance understanding and trust rather than promote the common atmosphere of distrust which comes from constant sniping.

If you are a woman in management, you might make it a policy never to pass on secondhand criticism. Instead, you would suggest to complaining employees that they talk first to the other person involved, and only if they are unsuccessful on the personal level will you enter as a mediator.

This is putting a biblical value to work on the job. This is one possible element in the Christian leadership style that all believers should be developing in the workplace today. And this is one way a Christian woman can have a greater influence on her working colleagues.

Each time a fellow worker discovers that you will not gossip or use information you gain against her to promote yourself, real trust develops. When you gain the reputation of being fair, of listening to both sides, of being a peacemaker rather than stifling communication and causing conflict, people will seek you out when they are struggling with a problem or need advice.

Many opportunities to share Christ will grow out of your leadership integrity on the job.

Self-Esteem and Career

One of the reasons that both men and women fall into the trap of gossiping and cutting others down is that so many struggle with self-image. They need to bring others down to feel better about themselves. But Christian women know their worth in Christ. They do not have to put others down. They will not be crushed if another has success or is promoted.

Women in Christ realize that there is more to their placement in the work world than just the jobs they are accomplishing. They know that by God's sovereign will they have been placed where they are to minister to others and to share the gospel.

There should not be an all-consuming passion to move up. In fact, all career choices need to be examined in the light of God's guidance and Christian values. Men and women who have chosen to follow Christ have picked up the cross. Can men and women on a cross have a long-term career plan set in cement? We should be ready to stay where we are or be open to change if either choice means that we may be more effective for Christ.

Boredom and monotony are also common in the workplace today. But this should not be the daily experience of Christians. As believers we can see each day as a new opportunity to serve Christ. We can do monotonous tasks and still be excited and in tune with the new possibilities that God may open up for us at any time.

I should point out here that everything said about Christian behavior in the workplace is as pertinent for men as it is for women. And I know that men are at least as active as women in gossip, power play and all the other sins of the workplace. The focus here on women simply recognizes that they are in a special position of influence today and that they will benefit greatly by thinking clearly about who they are and how they want to behave to achieve the greatest impact for Christ.

Women Who Work in the Home

To this point we have been considering women who work outside the home. Now let us look at the witness of women who work in the role of homemaker.

One thing Christian mothers and homemakers can do is to encourage other women who choose not to pursue careers outside the home, affirming the unquestionably essential value of the work they do. Christian women understand this in a way that other women do not, and they can be a loving encouragement to young mothers and homemakers who feel put down by the current societal values that degrade them and tell them that they are wasting their lives in the meaningless and mundane.

I have not read a clearer contemporary statement of the importance of mothers and wives than that written by George Gilder in his book *Sexual Suicide*. He writes,

The central position of the woman in the home parallels her central position in all civilized society. Both derive from her necessary role in procreation and from the most primary and inviolable of human ties, the one between mother and child. In those extraordinary circumstances when this tie is broken—as with some disintegrating tribes—broken as well is the human identity of the group. Most of the characteristics we define as humane and individual originate in the mother's love for her children.

Deriving from this love are the other civilizing concerns of maternity; the desire for male protection and support, the hope for a stable community life, and the aspiration for a better future. The success or failure of civilized society depends on how well the women can transmit these values to the men, to whom they come less naturally. The woman's sexual life and how she manages it is crucial to this process of male socialization. The males have no ties to women and children—or to long-term community—so deep or tenacious as the mother's to her child. That is primary in society, all else is contingent and derivative. . . .

The woman's place in this scheme is deeply individual. She is valued for her uniqueness. Only a specific woman can bear a specific child, and her tie to it is personal and infrangible. When she raises the child she imparts in privacy her own individual values. She can create children who transcend consensus and prefigure the future; children of private singularity rather than "child development policy." . . .

One of the roles of the woman as arbiter, therefore, is to cultivate herself; to fulfil her moral, aesthetic and expressive being as an individual. There is no standard beyond her. She is the vessel of the ultimate values of the society. The society is what she is and what she demands in men. She does her work because it is of primary rather than instrumental value. The woman in the home with her child is the last bastion against the technocratic marketplace.[2]

The Christian woman in the home can celebrate her primary role in society as the stable center from which her values flow through her children into the future of our world. To the extent that women refuse to have and nurture children, to love and coax their men into the stable relational structures that allow them to contribute meaningfully to family life, we will be diminished as a civilized society. That much lies in the hands of the women of our day.

There will always be men and women in excessive numbers who are able to perform the job functions required to keep the wheels of our corporations turning. But society itself will crumble without the essential leadership of loving, effective mothers and wives in our homes. Everything of worth, and for which we deeply care, derives from the fact of motherhood. When all is boiled down to one essential element, that is the only element we cannot do without.

Mothers who are homemakers can be a great encouragement to other women who are discovering by the thousands that careers do not bring deep and essential meaning to their lives. They can be living testimonies to the fact that having and raising significant children is of central importance to modern civilization. Rooted in the biblical tradition, wives and mothers today can witness the truth of God's own priorities revealed in Scripture for men and women alike. God brings his power and support to Christian families. He pours out his blessing on those who boldly and faithfully choose to have and raise children.

By their committed lives, women choosing family and home management today will witness to the world—especially to other women—the deeper dimensions of meaning available for those who faithfully choose in this way to build for the future of the church and for the good of the world to come.

For Individuals or Groups

1. What should be the ultimate priority that guides the behavior of Christian women today?

2. Review some of the attitudes and behaviors mentioned in the chapter that, if followed by women today, might create opportunities to be a witness for Christ in the workplace.

Add to this list other ideas from your own experience.

3. Do you think a woman might not be reaching her potential as a leader if she simply adopts a male leadership style? Why or why not?

4. Read Matthew 18:15-17. Discuss how this biblical pattern for conflict resolution might be applied to problems in the workplace.

What difficulties do you foresee in trying to follow this pattern?

How might the difficulties be overcome?

5. How can Christian women in the home be a witness for Christ in our day?

6. Review the value statements at the end of the chapter that argue for the importance of the role of wife and mother.

What do you think is the significance of the woman's role in the home?

8

All Businesses Should
Be Service Stations

It is rare today in businesses, offices, schools or restaurants to find an employee who actually engages you in a personal way. There are few places you can go where you feel that anyone there really cares about you as a person.

The most disturbing thing is that the institutions known traditionally for human care, such as nursing homes, hospitals and churches, have in many cases become as impersonal as other institutions. This is a place where we have let the world squeeze us into its mold instead of having a transforming and redeeming effect on others (Rom 12:2).

Do you remember when gas stations were commonly called service stations, and the good service stations were those that placed customer service at the top of their priority list? *Self-service* describes us today. The fact is, if you're not prepared to serve yourself, you won't get what you need. And the perverse aspect of this trend is that major advertising campaigns are now devoted to trying to convince the American public that they're really better off doing everything for themselves.

In one series of ads for a major oil company a young woman jumps eagerly out of her car at the gas station and starts right in telling us how wonderful it is that she can pump her own gas, check her own oil and wash her own windows. Nobody gets in her way anymore or holds her back. Nobody bothers her by washing her windows for her. She does as much as she wants and leaves when she wants.

A twenty-four-hour quick-stop grocery-store chain has a similar ad campaign that exalts self-service as customer freedom. The ads tell us how wonderful it is to be free to pour our own coffee and soft drinks, and free to microwave our own frozen sandwiches.

The height of this impersonal trend is probably symbolized best by a major grocery chain in our city. They have now taken away from the clerks even the minimal opportunity they had to interact with customers at the end of the transaction. After your sale is rung up, the computer now takes over and says in its metallic tone, "Thank you for shopping at Safeway; have a nice day."

The Personal Touch

Judie and I had a pleasantly different experience when we went into a little flower shop in Boulder a few months ago. An older woman approached us first and spoke no English but made it clear that her daughter would be with us in a moment. When the daughter came, we had a most delightful time. She gave us the distinct feeling that we were somehow not being sold anything. The purpose of the interaction for this girl was obviously the sheer enjoyment of spending time with people who shared her love for beautiful plants and flowers. And she was most concerned with who we were and what would make us happy. She kept coming back to the idea of what we liked best, what we wanted the plants for and whether the plants would thrive in the environment we would choose for them.

After about fifteen minutes, we made a couple of selections and she rang up our purchase. When I asked what identification she would need for the check she just took it and smiled and said, "That's fine." As we picked up our plants and started walking out, she called us back and said, "Wait. These are for you too." Her mother came out of the back with a small but beautiful bouquet of freshly cut flowers as a gift.

We had no idea whether these people knew Jesus or not, but after experiencing such personal care in that flower shop, Judie and I both remarked that if Christian business people would deal again in real service, putting people and their needs in the center focus, there would be a tremendous opportunity for Christ in our day. We talked about the experience all the way home. If people normally walked away from businesses or offices feeling the way we felt and the word got out that these places were owned or managed by Christians, what a difference this could make! If we will be person-centered in an impersonal world, we will be the aroma of Christ.

Jesus was person-centered. You cannot read the Gospels without realizing that people were his number one priority. The Pharisees, in comparison, were often duty- and issue-centered. A main contention between Jesus and the Pharisees was Jesus' apparent disregard for legalistic observances when these observances stood in the way of ministering to the needs of people. Jesus healed on the sabbath the man with the withered hand (Mt 12:9-14). On another occasion, when Jesus' disciples picked and ate grain on the sabbath, they were challenged by the Pharisees. Jesus answered by saying, "The Sabbath was made for man, not man for the Sabbath" (Mk 2:27).

Jesus also condemned the Pharisees for finding loopholes in the law that would protect them from having to act on their personal moral responsibilities to those around them. In the first part of Matthew 15 he exposes their common practice of dedicating material possessions to the temple so they could continue to enjoy the proceeds of their property instead of using their wealth to care for their parents.

In other places Jesus focused emphatically on the fact that attention to program had undermined the more fundamental need to love people. It was sinful, he said, for the Pharisees to pay close attention to cleanliness rituals (like washing dishes and cups properly) while ignoring the poor and hungry in their midst. It was sinful to maintain a minutely detailed tithing program while neglecting the deeper matters of justice and the love of God. It was sinful to preach the law that weighed heavily on people's shoulders while being unwilling to lift a finger to help those who were so burdened (Lk 11:37-46).

This chapter is not on the moral disease of the Pharisees, but these examples do show Jesus' constant and pervasive focus on the importance of loving people by meeting their needs, and his contempt for the practice of legalistically following programs that blind us to the real needs of those around us.

Similar problems still occur in the church. I knew a pastor, for instance, who refused to take communion to a dying Christian man who had requested it because their denominational polity taught that communion was a sacrament of the gathered body and not an individual event. When issues or office rules become more important to us than loving people, we make the mistake of the Pharisees, and Jesus' condemnation can rightly fall on us.

It always surprises me that Christian business people can be acutely aware of the need to be person-centered and have a person-centered ministry in the church, but they are often inept at transferring the importance of this concept into their own offices. I remember one businessman in our church who always pressed for a warm atmosphere in the church office and plenty of open space where conversation could happen easily. He strongly maintained that the receptionist should be a gregarious and sensitively relational person, without a huge pile of work to do. The receptionist had to be free to attend to the needs of those who came in.

But in his own office things were quite different. A young woman who worked there came to see me about the problems she faced at her job. As a Christian herself, she had a hard time reconciling the fact that the principal partners claimed to be Christians but had no apparent concern for their employees. In addition, they had no regard for their clients other than a financial one. She said the relational and caring network was so nonexistent there that her best friend could have committed suicide during the night, and there is no way anyone in that office would have ever found out about it.

If committed Christians like this woman have to struggle to keep their faith intact in businesses, schools, hospitals and restaurants run by their fellow Christians, what effect must those organizations be having on unbelievers?

Making a Personal Focus Work

A friend of mine has an office with about fifteen employees. It is a person-centered office where more attention is paid to the development of the human potential in the office than to the concern for making money. My friend suggests that the family-feel in the office, the inclusive way that issues and problems are handled, gives everyone the sense of their importance to the organization. They have a monthly lunch together, all fifteen of them. They take the time to creatively celebrate birthdays and other important personal events. And they have special days like their "office fish," where everyone goes to a lake and spends the day fishing, snacking, talking and having fun. Do they ever get any work done? My friend says the commitment level is higher than it ever could be with a pure money motivation. You can make money anywhere, but you can't find a family to work with five days a week. These fifteen people will do anything to ensure that their work is a success. Too much is at stake to let it go down the drain.

This same office creatively uses its expertise in landscape architecture and development to reflect a Christian commitment. For instance, they recently worked on a development project in an agricultural community in eastern Colorado. Older farmers and ranchers wanted to retire from their work but stay in the community. From the start, the retirement project was aimed at meeting the needs of these older people with high-security, low-maintenance town houses built on one level.

The office has also recently donated its architectural expertise to create a site plan and long-term development proposal for a Christian camp nearby. They saw the potential in the camp that others would not have seen.

All of this makes the point that our Christian businesses can and should take creative risks to reflect Christian principles in their management styles and project choices. This is one way Christians in business can communicate the truth of the gospel to those their businesses touch.

Another man in real estate does more than a financial tithe. He dedicates a tenth of his real estate holdings to be set aside for the Lord's work. This means that every tenth apartment, for instance, is used to house an individual or family who could not afford individual housing in any other way. The stories of how God has worked through this generous approach to a normally cutthroat real estate business are amazing.

Several attorneys I know take cases regularly for which they have no hope of financial gain. One recently responded to a request from a Christian friend who knew a young woman accused of abusing her son. The woman could not afford good legal counsel. Even after coming to suspect that the woman was guilty, my friend volunteered to represent her. When he told the judge he would handle the case, the judge criticized him publicly. He told him from the bench that he thought he was involved in too many gratis cases, and he didn't understand how he could support his private practice. Perhaps this is the reputation all Christian attorneys ought to have.

Another friend of mine in estate planning dedicates a portion of his time to people who are in debt over their heads. He helps them sort out their finances and get back on the track of sound management. He also searches for creative ways to arrange loans for those in need, often getting the needed funds from other clients who want to do something more with their money than just make more money.

Recent books like *In Search of Excellence* and *A Passion for Excellence* show that the most successful companies have found ways to incorporate the principles of caring and serving into their employee and customer interaction. Christians ought to be writing these books. We have known all along that people are significant and ought to be treated properly. We have known all along that people are more important than issues or programs, and that loving and caring about people is the only thing that will ever make a lasting difference in their lives.

Businesses and organizations managed and owned by Christians should be different. People working in and patronizing these organizations should sense that somebody up there loves them. And if they know they are truly loved by God's people, they will be more open to receiving the true source of love, Jesus Christ.

Caring and serving people as we relate to them in our businesses and jobs is another immensely important way Christians today can make the love of Christ known in a world that wonders why anyone in a business setting would take the time to relate personally in a significant rather than surface manner.

For Individuals or Groups

1. What recent experiences have you had with businesses or offices where you have been badly treated?

How could people in these businesses have handled things differently, leaving you with a positive rather than negative impression?

2. What is one of the best experiences you've had in dealing with a company, office or institution?

What made the experience a good one for you?

3. What principles can you transfer from the good experience you have had to the way you would like to treat others in your own work situation?

4. What principles have you learned from this chapter that you could apply to your office, business or your personal relational style at work that would communicate more fully the high regard you have as a Christian for people?

5. What step can you take in the next week to show Christ in the workplace?

9
Creative Excellence and Quality Products

There is a pervasive lack of concern for craftsmanship and quality products in our country today.

The Christmas gift exchange highlighted this reality for our family again this past year. We experienced the normal, even expected, deficiency of products—a skateboard that lost half its screws and bolts the first day, an expensive watch with a snap-on watch band that wouldn't stay snapped, and a host of other small but frustrating problems like pieces missing from games, toys and appliances that would not operate as effectively as advertised, and items damaged right out of the box.

Christmas only highlights this constant and widespread problem. All of us today are experiencing this increase in shabby workmanship and rapid decline in concern for quality products. Few of us will even carry an item out of a store anymore without unpackaging it first and thoroughly looking it over for defects.

Someone told me recently of a study which found that over seventy per cent of American workers surveyed said they would not buy the product they personally helped produce. The study also revealed that an equally large number of health and other service-related professionals would not choose to stay in the institutions for which they work. Nurses that would not admit themselves to their own hospitals when sick. Nursing-home professionals who would not place one of their own parents in the home where they work. This is a tragic state of affairs that should worry all of us.

There is one positive aspect, though, to this national reality. Here is another new opportunity in our day for Christians to witness who they are and what they believe by producing excellent products and standing behind what they sell.

Paul wrote, "Whatever you do, work at it with all your heart, as working for the Lord, not for men, since you know that you will receive an inheritance from the Lord as a reward. It is the Lord Christ you are serving" (Col 3:23-24). Christian men and women have good reason to do the best work possible.

The world does not understand the Christian concept of work. One modern bumper sticker reads, "I owe, I owe, so off to work I go." The thought behind the bumper sticker is that making money is the only reason a person would work. But for Christians, work has the deeper significance of becoming a daily act of worship and service to God.

Udo Middelmann expresses the unique nature of work for the Christian when he writes, "We are called on as Christians to be men before God, to have character, to fulfill the purpose of our creation which is to glorify God by being the ones he has made us to be. All of this is linked with expressing into the external world by the creative activity of work something of our identity as men."[1]

We are God's. We are created in his image. Our own creativity is a reflection of God's creative nature at work within us. Our work becomes a primary way we tell the world about our origin in and our allegiance to God in Christ. This is how work becomes worship for the Christian. When our work is marked by creative excellence, by concern for quality craftsmanship, by a real hope that it will serve others well, it glorifies God and proclaims God's nature and worth to the world.

Our good work is a witness for Jesus. Whether we produce a product or serve others in our work, the quality of what we do and the care we put into it will speak to those who buy our goods or receive our services that something other than the values of the world is at work within us. This is another important way that Christians can become the aroma of Christ in the world today.

There are four important aspects connected with our work that can set us apart as Christians. The first is our capacity to unleash the creative imagination of God on the problems of the world. Christians should be known as creative thinkers, their work marked by imaginative excellence. Second, the Christian will have a deep concern for the highest quality of craftsmanship. The quality of our work speaks of the quality of our God. Third, Christian men and women will be known for standing behind their products or services with an unusual degree of fairness and honesty. And finally, a Christian will advertise products honestly and fairly, not manipulating persons to consume products on the basis of emotional response to clever advertising technique. These are the four characteristics that are generally lacking in the secular world of production and service today.

Creative Excellence

Christians have an opportunity to witness today by being at the forefront in applying creative energy and thinking to the problems that confront people.

Think of the resources that are ours in Christ. Paul praises God at the end of Ephesians 3 as the one "who is able to do immeasurably more than all we ask or imagine, according to his power that is at work within us . . ." Not just able to do what we ask, or even what we can imagine, but able to do through us immeasurably *more* than anything we can possibly imagine.

As believers, we have the capacity to be open vessels for the creative energy of God to flow through us into the world. There should be a marked difference in the quality of life at the end of the twentieth century because Christians live in the world and work to enhance the quality of life.

What we choose to think creatively about should also be distinctive. Although nothing is outside the realm of God's concern, Christians should be known and recognized for their focus on human need, attacking the world's problems with solutions energized by the love of God. We should see Christians dealing with issues that relate to justice, hunger, the environment, the significance of human life.

But in any work we may do—whether in technology or art, in physics or theology—we can communicate the love of Christ in the gospel by accomplishing focused, single-minded creative thinking that relies on God to meet the critical human needs of our present world.

Quality Products

Many of us have had the wonderful experience of owning something of real quality, something that says unequivocally that the person or firm responsible really cares about producing the finest.

Our first home spoke to us in this way. It was a simple home (achieving quality is possible in all ranges of value), but the workmanship was good and the materials used were of a consistently high grade. We felt good just being in the home. Someone who cared about quality had designed and built all the houses in our subdivision. Appreciation for the builder was a common topic on our block. After living there a while, we found out from one of the neighbors that the builder was a Christian. We were not surprised.

I have also had the pleasant and comforting experience of being served in the medical profession by Christian doctors and nurses who understand the broad implications of their chosen profession. Their product is as much loving service for those who are fortunate enough to be their patients as it is physiological health care. These men and women are known in the community both for their commitment to excellence in their profession, and for the true human concern that flows from their changed hearts in Christ.

I know that it is not easy in every work situation to contribute to a high-quality product. In my first factory job I worked in quality control and shipping. We made a plastic laminate product that was carefully measured in my department to make certain it was within the tolerance levels specified on the job order. I would always report discrepancies to the foreman. His normal, predictable response was, "Ship it. If they can't use it, they'll send it back."

This problem was a constant struggle for me all the while I worked in the plant. I chose to stay on because I felt I did have some influence. A number of changes occurred for the better while I was there. But it was terribly difficult for me to ship merchandise I knew was out of tolerance.

Each of us has to judge the effectiveness of his or her work by bringing biblical content to our job-related choices. My struggle was the question of witness. Did my responsibility to follow the orders of my foreman destroy my witness on the job? I decided that it did not in this case. Everyone I worked with was sensitive to my personal struggle. My reputation for carefulness and integrity was well known in the plant, even though my foreman did not share my views and I felt I had to act under his authority. My decision to stay on was not an easy one. Other Christians I know would have quit the job rather than submit to the poor business practices. I may have been wrong to stay. Many jobs in today's world involve this kind of value struggle.

When my wife Judie took a nurse's aide job in a nursing home, she was confronted on her first night with the problem of an elderly woman who would not eat her supper. Judie sat down and tried to talk with the woman. The woman babbled incoherently. Judie stayed for quite a while, trying to feed the woman in small spoonfuls, bit by bit. She got nowhere at first, but after some time and with a lot of verbal coaxing the old woman started to eat the tiny spoonfuls and swallow them. Just as Judie began to make some progress, the head nurse happened by. The nurse watched for a moment and then just said, "We have no time for that." She picked up a large syringe, filled it full of food, jammed it in the woman's mouth and squeezed. She said, "That's how you'll do it from now on." After the nurse left, Judie glanced back at the old woman. The woman looked up at her. A tear trickled down the side of her face.

We often find ourselves in situations where we know what we would prefer to do in Christian love, but are not able to do it because of authority structures or time limitations. Judie struggled with that job. She was overworked, and no one really had the time to do anything beyond providing the barest necessities for the elderly patients. She still felt, though, that her presence there did often give her an opportunity to share the love of Christ with someone.

Our whole family got involved. Judie would pick patients who had no family and received no visits, and we would take them out whenever we could. We went to church functions and picnics, anywhere that we could spend a few hours of relaxed time together. The time was so valuable to those men and women. We felt fortunate to be able to give so much with so little personal effort.

I remember, though, that Judie would often serve at a deeply sacrificial level, spending time with patients before or after work to do the things there was no time to do during working hours. Christ was able to work through her loving commitment in that difficult, tension-filled job assignment. That is probably the test each of us finally applies to our own work. It is the litmus test of God's love poured out in service to others.

It is not an easy task in our day to be committed to quality. I have known some Christian men and women with this commitment who have had tremendous success in their work and businesses. I have known others with the same commitment to quality workmanship and service who, because of their refusal to cut corners, have not been able to financially sustain their work. There are no guarantees regarding the success or failure of our work. The only guarantee we have as Christians is that our reputation for integrity and commitment to quality cannot be taken away from us.

We may be successful in business by holding high standards for quality in product and service, and this will witness to the world that our values have their origin in God. Or we may have to fold a project to keep from compromising our integrity. But this too will say something powerful about who we are. Our commitment to quality will witness to the world our faith in Christ.

Standing Behind Your Product

My wife once worked for a man who owned and operated an appliance store in Minnesota. This Christian man would not sell an inferior product in his store. He carried only the best and backed up everything he sold. People would choose to buy at his store, even at higher prices than they might find for the same merchandise at a department store chain, because they knew that anytime they had a problem, they would be treated fairly. This man had a widespread and well-deserved reputation throughout the community.

A Christian mechanic who works on my cars explained how he views a warranty agreement. He has a written six-month or six-thousand-mile guarantee on work done. This is evidently standard in automobile repair work. But he calls his agreement an "open-ended" warranty. He says that anytime he finds that his shop is at fault for something breaking down or not functioning as it should, he fixes the problem at no charge, whether it is within or beyond the time or mileage stipulation in the written warranty.

As I talked with him he told me about the difficulty he encountered with one of his mechanics. This particular man had worked at a number of other garages and was in the habit of repairing vehicles as cheaply as possible, his only standard being that the repair outlast the written warranty. My friend was not able to convince the man of the importance of doing the best possible work, and had to let him go.

Honesty in Advertising

We have discussed in other chapters the importance for Christians of maintaining standards that do not allow for deception or manipulative techniques.

If a Christian automobile dealer advertises low-interest financing, the customer should never find out that the money he saved in low interest was really built back into the car deal in some other way. Or if a customer is assured by a Christian businesswoman that the program he is buying has been tested in his situation and will do the job, he should not find out later from the manufacturer that the system was never intended to handle the load he gave it.

Christian-backed promotional material must be distinctively different. It should aim to enlist the mind rather than depend purely on an emotional response. It should have an internal integrity, promising only what it can actually produce, not invading the freedom of individuals by manipulating them into making unwise choices. It should be refreshing in its honesty, bringing some real light into the otherwise dark world of secular advertising. It is easiest to sell a fallen world through fallen methods. The real challenge for Christians in promotion today is to bring creative excellence and integrity to advertising, whether promoting products or promoting the Christian faith through the media.

I have had the experience of choosing to patronize a store that uses a Christian symbol in its advertising, expecting the best, but finding instead an inferior product or low standard of work. There is probably nothing worse than advertising our Christianity boldly to raise expectations when in reality we operate our businesses from the value base of the world. When we say we are Christians but have the aroma of the world on our work, we destroy the witness of Christ in the world. But when we are committed to excellence in production and stand behind our work, we are distinctive in the world today, and have the capacity of affecting the world for Christ. They will know we are Christians by our high-quality work in a world that no longer practices that value.

Christian-based promotion can have the effect of spreading the aroma of Christ in the world. We are promoting products and services, but we are also witnessing the distinctive values demanded by faith in Jesus Christ.

Christian Concern

There are a couple of related ideas to touch on before leaving this topic.

A Christian employer has a unique opportunity to witness Christian values by the way he or she perceives and organizes the work of employees. We understand that work is meaningful because it is an expression of the creative nature and energy of God flowing through us and into the world. With this understanding, Christian employers will try to provide all their employees with engaging work tasks which call on the creative imagination and energy of the individual.

Another factory job I once held was in a punch-press department. I remember walking past a woman who was running several thousand aluminum labels through her machine each hour. I asked her what the labels were for. She had no idea. There was some company name printed on the labels. She had probably punched out a hundred thousand labels in two days but had never once stopped to read the company name on the piece. A Christian employer in an assembly-line plant like that has a real challenge. How can the tasks be assigned and accomplished in such a way that the humanity of employees is retained at the highest possible level?

In our fallen world not all job assignments can enlist a creative response, but most can be organized in such a way that they become more meaningful for those on the job. Putting a high premium on employee participation in company decisions is another way to show that you hold the value of persons very high. This kind of employer can have a great impact for Christ today.

A second sidelight worthy of mention is that the current lack of quality in products means that most of us will be taking items back to the store on a fairly regular basis. The understanding and forgiving attitude we have as we return faulty merchandise to the store can be like a breath of fresh air to clerks who deal all day long with nothing but angry, disgruntled customers.

Think of the impact Christians across the country could have if by the thousands we returned merchandise with a smile, having real human concern for what a difficult job it must be for these clerks to listen to constant complaining eight hours a day, five days a week. I am certain the Lord could work through our kindness, understanding and good humor in these situations. It is worth thinking about.

The principles outlined above are just Christian common sense. But it is easy for us to lose our concentration in life, to become chameleons, changing our values to meet the world situations in which we find ourselves.

Our prayer together can be that we will be able to maintain a consistent focus on who we are and what we believe and how that affects us daily in our work. Our hope is that we will not compromise our faith and consequently compromise our witness in the world.

For Individuals or Groups

1. What is the meaning of work for Christians?

2. The author lists four important aspects connected with our work that can set us apart as Christians. Review and summarize these four aspects.

Which of these four needs the most attention where you work? Explain.

3. What problems will an employer face if he or she takes seriously the importance of trying to provide meaningful and creative work opportunities for employees?

How can these be overcome?

4. If you have a monotonous, assembly-line type of job that offers no outlet for your creative expression in work, how might you satisfy your longing to do creative work by pursuing other interests during your free time?

5. Think of one conflict you regularly experience because your job requires you to compromise some value you hold as a Christian worker. Is there anything you can do to improve this situation? If so, what?

10
Trusting and Being Trustworthy

T*wo members of our congregation moved their busi-*ness into a new office building in town. They noticed that their neighbors in the office across the drive had a volleyball court. They thought it would be fun to get to know them by having the two offices play some volleyball together.

When they contacted the other office, the reception was cool. Someone would call them back in a couple of days to let them know. About a week later they received a call from the other company's attorney. He told them that they couldn't let them play a game of volleyball with their company because of the liability factor of the net being on their property.

My friends made it clear that they would even sign a release form if it would allow the two offices to get together for a friendly game and a chance to meet each other. The lawyer told them the only way it would work was if they would take out a special insurance policy to cover themselves in case of an injury.

Something has gone wrong in our country when two offices can't even play a friendly game of volleyball without worrying about special liability insurance. And isn't it amazing as well that we have to deal with attorneys on almost any issue that comes up today?

Is it really impossible to do business today on the basis of trust? Or can Christians be more trusting—even though there are risks involved—and say something significant about who they are as they take a posture of trust amid the twisted attitudes of suspicion and defensiveness that mark our world today?

Trust: Wise but Defenseless

Christians should be a people of trust. Their lives are rooted in Christ. They are freer than their neighbors in the world who are frightened, worried and constantly working to protect themselves from every angle in their quest for earthly security.

Our security is in Christ. It is not in our businesses or in our money or in our possessions or in any other thing. We do not have to protect ourselves any longer because God is our protector.

Jesus said to his disciples, "I am sending you out like sheep among wolves. Therefore be as shrewd as snakes and as innocent as doves" (Mt 10:16). The picture is one of wise but defenseless disciples. They are wise in that they shrewdly seek to discern God's will as they work in the world for Christ. They are innocent in that they, like sheep, cannot defend themselves. But they do not need to. In doing the will of God, they have God's protection. The sheep are always protected by the Good Shepherd.

Each of us will have to struggle to find the way to hold a reasonable regard for the resources God has placed in our trust, while at the same time we display a righteously carefree attitude of trust that can mark us as Christians in the world today.

There are no guarantees that we will not be ripped off if we risk trusting others. Christians are robbed, raped, exploited. The only promise we have is that there is nothing in heaven or on earth that can separate us from the love of Christ (Rom 8:31-39). And knowing this should make a difference in the way we relate to those around us in this area of trust.

We can start out with small things and work our way up. Being willing, for example, to lend out tools, let someone borrow our cars, bring strangers into our homes, are all fairly low-risk ways that we can begin to trust others more.

In business our beginning choices may be something like not asking for identification on checks. Or it may mean not having a multitude of protective devices in our stores that say that we expect everyone around us to steal. If we can create an atmosphere in our personal and business lives that communicates trust rather than suspicion, it will make a huge difference in how our neighbors and customers relate to us. This can be an open door for Christ to work.

A woman I know who owns a number of properties tells me that since she started writing loose agreements with her tenants and stopped collecting huge damage deposits, she has seen a tremendous increase in the care tenants give her properties. She has also had many opportunities to share the gospel because her basic posture of trust is so different from the protective stance of other landlords.

If someone does take advantage of us, the choices we make regarding forgiveness and the manner in which we work out sticky problems can also testify to the fact that we are ruled by the love of Christ instead of the love of our things.

A number of years ago, while riding home from work on my motorcycle, I was hit broadside by a young man who ran a stoplight. My bike was destroyed, but I was miraculously all right, except for a number of bad bruises and a broken ankle.

The young man who ran into me had no insurance. I was angry about the immature way he handled his affairs, and I was not surprised to learn that he had a great deal of difficulty finding and keeping a job. He was now in deep trouble with the law for driving without insurance and for running the red light.

The young man felt badly about the accident, and to his credit, he called regularly to see how I was getting along. I thought it would be right for him to have to pay the damages, but I chose not to bring extraordinary pressure to bear on him. I worked with him in his difficult situation and gave him adequate time to set things straight.

The young man took a job as soon as he could find one. He started paying me back right away for damages to my motorcycle and making regular payments to my insurance company for the medical bills. He made little money, and he chose to keep only a small portion of it for himself until he made things right.

A few months after I'd gotten the cast off my leg, I was dressing one morning in the locker room at a city recreation center. One of the men near me saw the ugly scars on my leg and asked what happened. I briefly told him the story. I'll never forget his response. He said, "I'd have had that guy paying me for the rest of his life."

I knew with certainty that day that there is a striking difference between the world's way and the way of God's people. My hope was that the young man who ran into me would realize when he thought about it that the end of his story might have been different if he had hit someone else. Yes, I probably could have sued and received a large, long-term settlement from this accident. But what positive effect could have resulted regarding the possible redemption of this young man if I had chosen that avenue?

A modern business magazine published a story recently on a Christian man in Warrendale, Pennsylvania, who decided to try something different in his restaurant. Instead of putting prices on the menu, Juliano decided to ask the customers to pay what they thought the food was worth. "I didn't do it to make the business any greater," Juliano explained. "I think the Lord guided me to do it to show people they should trust one another."

The amazing thing is that, without prices, sales have increased twenty-five per cent, and business is booming at the restaurant. The article reports that Juliano expects to be ripped off from time to time. But the amazing thing is that only two customers have eaten at the restaurant without leaving any money. Juliano was pleased, though, that even those customers ate everything they were served.[1]

A Christian resort in Colorado has tried something similar. They open their doors to everyone without charge. The registration card suggests a cost per person of staying at the lodge with all meals included. But the card makes it clear that people should pay what they are able and what they think the stay is worth. The manager told me that some cannot afford to pay much, but many others give far beyond the suggested cost of the stay to help make up the difference. In this way, families that could never afford to stay anywhere else are given an opportunity for a restful time together at a beautiful Colorado mountain lodge.

Businesses like these show the world that it is possible to operate on a different scale of values. How many eating at Juliano's or staying at that Christian lodge have had to honestly confront the reality of the Christian faith because of the loving and trusting treatment they have received?

Being Trustworthy

Another way Christians today can have salvation appeal is by being trustworthy.

Paul says that church leaders should "have a good reputation with outsiders" (1 Tim 3:7). But it does not just pertain to leaders, for the early church in the book of Acts is described as "enjoying the favor of all the people." A positive relationship with the community was so strong that "the Lord added to their number daily those who were being saved" (Acts 2:47).

Christians should be people for whom a handshake and their word still mean something. Christians should be people who can be trusted. Christians will not take advantage of someone sexually. This would be contrary to the law of love. Christians should be faithful, honest and fair with employees today. And Christians will be honest in trade, not given to false advertising or shady schemes, and will stand behind their products or service with a moral commitment, not just a legal warranty agreement.

An automobile mechanic rebuilt an engine for me. Two years later I had a problem with the engine. I had put twenty-five thousand miles on the rebuilt engine, nineteen thousand miles beyond the upper limit of the warranty agreement. The man was a Christian. When he looked at the engine, he could find nothing that had been improperly done, but he told me his work should last longer than twenty-five thousand miles, and he would split with me the cost of rebuilding the engine again. This kind of treatment should be the mark of Christians in business today. It speaks highly about who Jesus is and why someone might want to find out more about him.

Reading Samuel's farewell speech that ushered King Saul into leadership (1 Sam 12) would be a good reminder to all of us of the honesty that should mark our lives. Samuel says, "Here I stand. Testify against me in the presence of the LORD and his anointed. Whose ox have I taken? Whose donkey have I taken? Whom have I cheated? Whom have I oppressed? From whose hand have I accepted a bribe to make me shut my eyes? If I have done any of these, I will make it right" (v. 3). The people reply, "You have not cheated or oppressed us. You have not taken anything from anyone's hand" (v. 4). These verses are a great challenge to us today. We should live lives worthy of the calling to which we have been called. Christians should be trustworthy. And if we can be trusted, people will seek us out, and we may have an opportunity to point them toward the one who is the reason for our behavior.

I have been impressed also with the stories of Christian men and women who have made serious mistakes but were willing to consider restitution for these. Samuel said, "If I have done any of these, I will make it right."

One Christian man I knew went bankrupt in real estate owing millions. He tried at first simply to put it all behind him. He began working for a well-known Christian evangelistic association. After working full-time for the Lord for many years, he became convinced that God was asking for restitution. He went back into the real estate business, and God blessed him greatly. It took nearly a decade, but he eventually paid back every cent of his enormous debt.

Imagine being one of this man's creditors. After fifteen or eighteen years, you suddenly find a check in your mail for the total amount owed from that almost forgotten bad debt. There is also a note enclosed. The man simply asks for forgiveness and tells how God would not let him rest until he paid back those he owed.

If Christians can be a people of trust in a world of suspicion, they will have an impact for Christ. If they can be prepared to accept the consequences of living out a life marked by loving trust in others, the message that love is more important than self-protection will turn some. These will be drawn by the aroma of Christ in Christians who trust and are trustworthy. This is a challenging but worthwhile aim for all of us concerned with sharing the love of Christ in our needy world.

For Individuals or Groups

1. If our security is in Christ, what difference should this make in the way we trust those around us?

2. Why does the author believe that as Christians we should not spend an excessive amount of time trying to protect ourselves?

3. Explain what you think it means to have a "righteously carefree attitude of trust. . . ."

4. Review the ideas mentioned in this chapter on how businesses can take a stronger trusting posture and have an impact for Christ. What ideas can you add to this list?

5. The world powerfully influences the behavior of all of us today. What are some

of the ways Christian men and women may give in to the world's way and, by doing so, hurt their witness of credibility and trustworthiness?

6. Name one area in which your trustworthiness (or lack of it) could damage your good reputation as a Christian. What do you believe God would have you do in this area?

7. If we have blown it by making bad choices and by behaving inappropriately as Christians, how might these bad situations still be redeemed and have the effect of honoring Christ?

11
Christians and the Abuse of Power

I have the power!" He-Man says.

He is a favorite superhero for children today. We learn to appreciate at an early age what it means to have and wield power and, unfortunately, with often devastating clarity, what it means to be without power.

Nietzsche is attributed with the saying, "Basic to the human personality is the will to power." He is right. And we might add an inductive truth, "Basic to the structure of human organizations is the will to power." Every aspect of our society—business, politics, education, religion, marriage and family as well as other relational institutions—operates largely on the basis of power.

I will never forget the first major job interview I had with the superintendent of a large school district in Minnesota. He was the last of a string of people with whom I had to interview, but it was clear that he had the final say.

His office was designed in such a way that when I walked in and stood in front of him on the lower level, he could look me straight in the eye from a sitting position on the upper level behind his huge, kidney-shaped desk. His own desk chair was plush, tall and straight-backed. When I sat in the slant-backed, smaller chair on the lower level, I was a full two feet below him, looking up. The impression of power given by the furniture arrangement alone was intense. It was a devastating thought that so much of my life's preparation, education and work toward my goals was now tied up in the fingers and pen of this one power-conscious individual.

My experience was certainly not unique in today's world. Every one of us deals daily with the use and abuse of power. Power is the way of the world. But how should Christians view the use of power? What parameters does our theology of love place upon the use of power? And what effect might we have on those around us if we refuse the temptation to use the power of the world in our relationships or workplace? Jesus had some interesting things to say about the power of the world.

Mark describes in detail in his Gospel the story of James and John coming to Jesus with a request. They wanted the Lord to allow one of them to sit at his right and one at his left when he achieved his glory (Mk 10:35-45). It is a compelling story. When the other disciples heard of the request they were immediately angered. It is apparent that their irritation did not spring from righteous motives. Each one was secretly convinced that he was the most deserving of the number one spot, ahead of the rest. The disciples often argued with one another about who was the greatest (Mk 9:34).

Jesus called them to himself using a warm, parental gesture, and made several important points about power and position. First, he said that there are two distinct styles of leadership, the world's style and the kingdom's style. He said the rulers of the world lord it over their subjects, dominating them through power. But Jesus was quick to point out that it must not be this way in the kingdom of God. The mark of leadership in God's kingdom is servanthood, not title, position or the use of power. The kingdom leader must be willing to be last for the sake of all, actually the "slave" of all.

Jesus then said that his own life was the example for kingdom leadership. Even the Son of man came to serve, not to be served, and to give his life for others. We immediately think of Philippians 2 in this regard. Jesus emptied himself, took on the form of a slave. Of what did he empty himself? Glory! Yes, and power!

I have become convinced that we cannot have it both ways. Love and power will not march together. If we are acting in power, we will not be expressing love. If we are acting in love, we will not be expressing negative power. This is a crucial point for Christians concerned with sharing Christ in the world today. It is the reason why Christians who bomb abortion clinics or shoot the publishers of pornographic magazines will have no positive effect in the world for Jesus Christ. If we are depending on the world's power to achieve our ends, we will not be living in love. And it is love, not power, that will win the world for Christ.

The essential lifestyle choice we have as Christians is between choosing a committed style of love and giving in to the world's use of manipulative power. Will we operate from a power base? Or will we be rooted and grounded in love? In *Power and Innocence: A Search for the Sources of Violence,* Rollo May gives a helpful analysis of several possible kinds of power. He calls his first type of power *exploitive.* This is the power of sheer force. It is the use of physical violence to overpower others and render them helpless. This is the Hell's Angels style of human interaction.

The next kind of power May identifies is *manipulative* power. This is the psychological power of the con artist who seeks to control through covert methods. James Bond is a good example. He always makes the woman fall in love with him, but he never falls in love with her. This puts him in the position of least interest, having more power over her than she does over him. He can use the women who fall in love with him for his own advantage.

A third kind of power is *competitive* power. This power has both positive and negative sides. Competition can and does lead to greater achievement. But normally the presupposition here is that if I am going to move upward, I need to step on or put down others. Only one person can really be the winner.

A fourth kind of power is what May calls *nutrient* power. This is power for others, such as a mother's care for her own children. The negative side of this kind of power is "smother" love in which a person creates through the use of this power a dependent rather than an independent relationship. If I can make someone dependent upon me, I have control over that person.

A final kind of power mentioned is *integrative* power. This is described by May as power with others that seeks to gain something for the community, empowering others to grow and mature fully in any life dimension.

This is certainly the kind of power that Jesus himself demonstrated throughout his life. He sensitively sought to empower others with the means to effectively manage their own lives under God. Jesus did not use power against others but demonstrated that love empowers others to be all they can be. He refused to take advantage of another's weaknesses. Instead, he encouraged strengths and acted in the power of love to empower others to follow his loving example.

Christians must say no to the temptation to use any manipulative or coercive power. Jesus said we were to follow his example of kingdom leadership. Then he gave us a picture of what he expected from those of us who are his. He took the basin and towel and knelt to wash the feet of his disciples. This is the kind of loving action that will make a difference in our competitive and power-hungry world. Many of our neighbors and coworkers long to experience something more in life than the struggle of competition and the fear and defensiveness that comes from the long-term struggle to survive in the world of power. By loving our neighbors and refusing to use power against them, Christians can be the aroma of Christ today, helping those around them to find their way to Jesus through the draw of the power of love.

What are some of the specific ways we as Christians can refuse to use or abuse power, and so become living examples of the better way of love?

Christian Organizations and the Corporate Use of Power

First, it is important for the church and for parachurch groups to pay attention to the power impression they give through the choices they make. The church and other Christian organizations can begin to look and act power hungry.

Jerry Falwell, Pat Robertson, Jim Bakker, Oral Roberts and others are often criticized for using manipulative fund-raising techniques to drive their Christian empires. Many good things are accomplished through these ministries, but when they employ the power techniques of the world to fund their work, we can expect diminishing returns.

It is important, for instance, to consider how building a crystal cathedral in our day will impact those who do not know Christ. Is this an appropriate symbol for the church in today's world? Or does this power image bring too much of the world into the church, confusing unbelievers and creating a stumbling block that keeps them from responding to the gospel?

Much of what Christians do today in a corporate sense looks suspiciously like self-centered empire building. And when a Christian leader begins to send the message that he might be more interested in adding floors to his hospital or university than he is in helping and caring for the people in these institutions, it leaves the wrong taste in everyone's mouth.

When a popular TV evangelist today has his own name embossed in large gold letters on the Bibles he sells, it is an indication that something has gotten out of perspective. Compare that action to Ken Taylor's personal refusal to take any money from the sale of *The Living Bible* and *The Book*. Which action carries with it more of a sense of the presence of the Spirit of Christ?

Caution is needed. There is a real danger in the subtle, twisted logic of the world of power. It is easy to begin to believe that the ends justify the means in our important projects for God. But this is never true for those who belong to Christ.

And what do churches do when they get into trouble financially or in some other way. Do they trust God? Or do they use the manipulative power techniques of the world to solve their problems? We have to ask seriously whether it might be better to let a Christian organization fold than to give in to a questionable use of power to pump it up.

The drive to succeed in an organizational sense is a power drive borrowed from the world and rooted in the pride of human achievement. We have all heard of power plays made in struggling churches, and even of illegal financial decisions endorsed by desperate pastors. This is a sure way to take on as a corporate body the smell of the world rather than to have the aroma of Christ. And it will kill attempts to reach people with the gospel. We cannot express power and love at the same time.

Experience tells us that God is not as concerned with whether we succeed or fail in any particular project as he is with how we meet our successes and failures. And when unbelievers today observe how we meet our successes and failures with Jesus Christ, it is often the most compelling witness we have.

Everything said here about the quest for power, empire building and the success motivation in life applies as well to individual Christians as it does to corporate Christian entities.

The Success Motivation in Life

Nothing more clearly indicates the extent to which we have let the world squeeze us into its mold than our use of power to get to the top in the businesses or institutions in which we work. Christians have only one good choice. If we cannot gain promotions or maintain our positions through diligence, fairness and creative quality of performance, we must be willing to give up our jobs in order to maintain our integrity.

I have always admired a good friend of mine who was drafted into the Yankee baseball organization out of college and began working his way up through the farm system. He told me that the intense competition and the power games played on and off the field made it incredibly difficult to work one's way up. Using manipulative techniques to draw attention to oneself while downplaying the talents of others appeared to be the only way to move.

My friend quit his dream just this side of the big time. His view was simple—you could say, simply Christian. What good did it do to gain the world if it meant losing his soul?

Power is subtle. Like many Christian men and women following dreams, I had my own dream once of making it big with a Christian rock group. The group I played with recorded on A & M records and booked with the William Morris Agency out of Chicago. We played with all the big name groups in the late sixties and early seventies. But as we moved up in the world of music, we became aware of some changes occurring in our songs. Suddenly it seemed appropriate to us to tone down the direct Christian message that had been our mark as a group. We began writing more songs that were upbeat and had a general rather than specific message. The general message was more marketable. We told ourselves that we could compromise a little now in order to get into a stronger position to have a greater effect for Christ later. In the world of power the ends always seem to justify the means. The truth is, when we begin to sell ourselves to power, power gains a greater and greater hold on us. We become slaves to power.

At one point when the group's recording and agency contracts both came up for renewal, we took a week to pray, think and discuss where we were and where we were heading. We chose at the end of that time not to sign the contracts that would have tied us into the secular music industry for several more years. It is always heart-rending to give up a dream. But to obtain a life's dream through compromising our integrity as Christians would never lead to inner satisfaction, joy and peace. These qualities that all of us desire will only be ours if we can deny power, if we in fact hold power over power.

The witness of our refusal to use and abuse people or to compromise our faith to achieve worldly success will be a tremendous statement today that there is a better way offered through faith in Christ.

Christian Media

A proper use of media is another way Christians can demonstrate a refusal to abuse power. When Christians fall prey to using the manipulative techniques of the world in Christian media, they shut off the possibility of reaching people for Christ. In this case, the medium really is the message.

We can talk all day about how much we love people, but when we say those words while at the same time trying to cleverly manipulate them through guilt or other techniques (especially when our goal is raising money), the real message comes through loud and clear. You can fool some of the people some of the time, but in the end, the misuse of power will not bear fruit for the kingdom of God.

Recently we showed a series of films in our congregation on the origin of life and evolution. We rented the films because of the advertising that promoted them as balanced, factual presentations. When the films were shown, we realized that the Christian producers were using a wide variety of clever techniques borrowed from secular films and advertising to sway the thinking of the audience toward their own often loosely founded theories. All of the things we Christians complain about in secular presentations—shallow thinking, sarcasm, lack of relevant evidence, blatant emotionalism— were common in these Christian films. We also thought the advertising we received on the film was misleading.

If the Christian position is true, then we should be able to present the Christian viewpoint in a reasonable way that engages thinking people. Christians ought to be able to do it better.

Another film I watched not long ago was an abortion film that began with a good presentation of both sides of the abortion argument. I was hopeful that the Christian producers of the film realized the importance of working on the issue rationally, and as the argument progressed I was certain that the sheer evidence being mounted would convince people of the importance of the pro-life stand. But to my dismay it soon became clear that the arguments presented at the beginning of the film were being used as a mere technique to draw people in. Once you were fully engaged in the argument, they suddenly switched gears and ended the film by showing three actual abortions taking place. Engage their minds, but then shock them emotionally with something they will never forget for the rest of their lives. I felt raped. My mind and emotions were manipulated. A dirty trick was played on me. And these were Christian people who were supposed to care about me.

What kind of message is communicated to the world when Christians use these kinds of power techniques in their attempts to persuade? Paul said to the Corinthians, "My message and my preaching were not with wise and persuasive words, but with a demonstration of the Spirit's power, so that your faith might not rest on men's wisdom, but on God's power" (1 Cor 2:4-5).

Christian advertisements should be the most honest pieces of promotion on the market today. Christian communication should be clear and effective, but free from the manipulative techniques that are prevalent in secular advertising. Christian films should be ruthlessly honest about the Christian life. It is the honesty and the fact that we care enough to tell the truth that will allow the Spirit to work and win people to Christ.

Christian media people who are trying to fight fire with fire are in a losing battle. We need to do it better, not just duplicate the methods of the secular world in media. The truth may not be as exciting initially as an emotionally manipulative technique, but it is still the truth, and it will wear better over time. The truth stirs the hearts of men and women. We need to fight fire with truth and love. People are tired of being manipulated through the media. When they see something different, they will recognize it and respond positively to it. A more honest Christian media will have a great impact for Christ today.

Sex and the Use of Sexual Power

Both sexes can have an impact for Christ by controlling the sexual power inherent in their relationships.

On the simplest level, I have known both men and women who have come to know Christ today through the experience of meeting a Christian under control, another man or woman who would not allow their relationship to experience the damage caused by the negative power of illicit sex. Chastity might be one of the best methods of evangelism available to us in our sexually promiscuous society. When sex is so easily obtained today, those who know and appreciate the deeper meaning of sexuality and refuse to cheapen this God-given reality will have a compelling mystery about them. God can work through this unusual obedience in our world today.

Most important in this area is the behavior of Christian men related to the dating games presently played in our culture. A shocking statistic came out of a study done at the University of South Dakota with a random sample of 408 women students. One in five of these women, 20.6 per cent, admitted to being raped on a date. Rape was clearly defined as being "physically forced by a dating partner to have sexual intercourse." Nearly half reported being sexually taken advantage of by men who held, kissed or fondled them against their will. And ten per cent said they had been physically abused by men on at least one occasion.[1]

What a tremendous impact Christian men can have today by treating women with the kind of loving respect due every person created in the image of God. Refusing to use physical or manipulative power in the sexual realm to take advantage of women will testify to a value system rooted in the love of Christ. The power games of spending money on women so they will feel obligated or manipulating through guilt and pressure should be totally off limits for the Christian man.

Women can also be guilty of using their sexual power to manipulate men to serve selfish needs. Again, Christian men and women should never play these kinds of power games. Integrity in the sexual area will bring trust, and trust will create an openness to considering the gospel.

In her book on power, Cheryl Forbes explores the more subtle influences of sexual power in the work world.[2] She says about male forms of abuse of sexual power, "We could rephrase 'barefoot, hungry, and pregnant' to read, 'keep them poorly paid, eager, and overworked.' "

Sexual harassment in the workplace takes many forms. Even though it is hardly ever stated openly anymore, a man is still often thought of as the "breadwinner" who needs more money to make ends meet in the family. Or women are passed up for promotions because men in the company would be threatened by such a move. And if women stand up to immoral and illegal treatment, they are immediately branded as hard to work with, demanding and unfeminine. And who in his right mind would want to promote someone like that to a higher position of power?

This is another place where Christian men can have a great influence today. They can recognize women who are creative, strong and skillful in their jobs, and work to promote these talented women fairly, without sexual bias. Refusing to use sexual power to freeze women at a level that poses no threat to men will be a remarkable stance for Christian men today. John taught that perfect love casts out fear. He was right. Because we are loved by Christ and choose to love as he loves us, Christian men can risk boldness today by refusing to misuse sexual power against women in business or family life.

Men who work to fairly promote qualified women will also help to break the traditional pattern of forcing women to use their sexual power as a way to gain recognition and promotion. Women should be free to be themselves, to concentrate creatively on their work. No one should have to try to work well while having to manage the nagging bitterness that creeps in when one is under the constant pressure of being unfairly treated.

This kind of openness between the sexes creates an atmosphere that can bring the aroma of Christ into the workplace. Recognizing that the men and women around us are God's finest creation and treating them accordingly will always have this effect of heightening the possibilities of right relating in an atmosphere of love.

The Power of Money

It is the frantic quest for earthly wealth that marks our society today. Enormous amounts of energy are poured into get-rich-quick schemes that play on the vain hopes of millions. State lotteries legalize gambling and take advantage of the natural human tendencies toward laziness, greed and easy answers. We receive sweepstakes promotions in the mail several times a month and spend enormous amounts of time and money hoping that we will somehow beat the 1 in 50,000,000 odds against us. We also believe that even though our neighbors were ripped off and did not receive the gift they had hoped to get by sitting through the high-pressure sell, it will somehow be different in our case. We are like B. F. Skinner's chickens which, when given the slot-machine type of intermittent reward, pecked relentlessly at the metal disk until they dropped from sheer exhaustion.

Our society is driven in its quest for money and the things money can buy. This turns out to be a quest for power: the power to be free from the unnecessary burden of work or the power to be free from worries about scarcity or the cost of unexpected tragic circumstances. And money has the power to open doors. People want that kind of power.

The catch is, of course, that money may have the effect of reducing tension in some areas, but it always increases tension in others. When you have money, you need to find ways to protect it. Money has a way of controlling us, and it is very difficult to gain control over its power. This is why the rich today are still one of the highest-risk groups for suicide.

Christians can live in marked contrast when it comes to the proper view and use of money. Few things will have a greater impact on those around us than our generous choices to use money to help others. The fact that we can give money away will be a testimony that we live with our roots in a different place.

The world knows that money is for hoarding, manipulating, spending lavishly on oneself. It is only given away as a method to gain power over others. So when Christians demonstrate that helping people is more important than having money, they make a strong statement about the peace and security of life in Christ.

It comes back again to this simple idea. If we value people above things and even above the power that money can bring, we will become the aroma of Christ to those who are being saved. The Bible has always been strong on this issue. People, not money, should be our first concern. This is why charging interest was not acceptable in Old Testament times. It was seen as taking advantage of a person who was experiencing hard times (Ex 22:25). There are many other biblical examples, but if we are to be witnesses in this area, we will think creatively about how to state clearly by our actions that people are a high priority while amassing wealth for ourselves is low on our list.

If we are in business, we will look differently at the wages we choose to pay. Situations of human need will be considered along with merit. We will be generous to employees without ever using our generosity as a manipulative technique to place workers in our debt. We will think of ways to include our employees in profit sharing. Our progressive and creative means of rewarding our employees will become known in the work world of our community. Christian businessmen and women have a great opportunity to demonstrate their faith in this area.

The fact that we lend tools to neighbors and are generous with the things God has provided for us is another way that we can live out our theology of money and have an effect for Christ. If something we own is returned damaged, we have an opportunity to show our neighbor in no uncertain terms that he is more important to us than this material thing we own. We should always be more concerned about maintaining a human relationship than we are about losing some money.

Finally, as Christians, we should never be guilty of treating one person more highly than another on the basis of whether he or she has money.

This may be the strongest witness we have. Everywhere in the world money opens doors for the rich that stay closed to the poor. If Christians are guilty of showing this kind of favor, they will smell more like the world than they will like Jesus. James harshly condemns this kind of favoritism (Jas 2:1-4). If we treat with respect and love those who are used to being mistreated in the world because they have not achieved a certain economic status, we will have a tremendous impact for Christ. If we are open doors for those who normally have doors slammed in their faces, Jesus will be effective through us.

Evangelism, Love or Power

Jesus refused to use the power of the world to achieve his ends. Satan's temptation of Jesus in the wilderness was an attempt to get him to use power to advance himself. He would not. Jesus knew the only power that would really achieve the blessed work of his Father was the power of the cross.

We will do well to remember this example when we share Christ with others. It is sacrifice, not coercion, that most closely matches the God-ordained method by which Jesus would win the world. It is the love of a life given up for others that engages the world and draws men and women to a life in Christ.

I remember standing with my daughter in a long line of people waiting to get into the Michael Jackson concert in Denver when a group of young Christians came past yelling and screaming Bible verses at people, condemning them in the name of Jesus to hell if they did not repent and turn from their wicked ways. This is the violence of coercive power that smells more like the world than it does like our loving Savior. We use guilt, condemnation, exclusiveness and a host of other violent methods to manipulate men and women into the kingdom of God. We have too many He-Man Christians in the body of Christ today.

If we, after the model of Jesus, give up our lives in love for others, we will reach more of our neighbors for Christ and have stronger converts than if we give in to manipulative techniques to try to force hasty spiritual decisions. We cannot express power and love at the same time. And it is love that will win the world for Christ.

For Individuals or Groups

1. The world is on a quest for power and success. What is the Christian's quest? What effect should this different motivation have on the way we live our lives?

2. What are some ways in which each of us gives in to the use of worldly power

in our everyday lives?

3. Pick one area of your life in which you tend to use the power of the world to accomplish your ends. How might you act differently in this area, modeling love instead of power?

4. Do you agree or disagree with the statement, "We should always be more concerned about maintaining a human relationship than we are about losing some money" (p. 115)? Explain.

5. What controls do the demands of love place on our methods of evangelism and outreach?

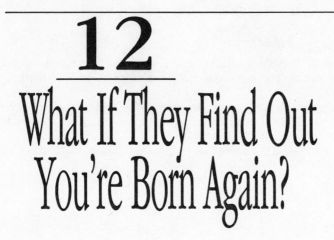

12

What If They Find Out You're Born Again?

I*f you practice some of the lifestyle suggestions made in* this book, sooner or later someone will discover that you are a Christian. What will you do then?

Proclamation Evangelism

Peter reminds us, "Always be prepared to give an answer to everyone who asks you to give the reason for the hope that you have" (1 Pet 3:15). Conforming our lives to the truth is not enough in itself to carry the entire task of evangelism in our day. We have to be able and willing to speak the truth as well as live it, and to close the loop when the opportunity to do so arises. When our neighbors ask us to clarify some aspect of our faith, or to tell them what they must do to be saved, it is important for us to be prepared to respond.

Proclamation evangelism is the verbal witness to the truth of the person and work of Jesus the Christ. It is a significant step in the evangelism process and cannot be left out. But we all would do well to remember that evangelism is a process which includes relational and verbal aspects. Neither aspect alone can do the whole job. We can develop an extraordinary relationship with someone we care about, but if we never tell that person what she needs to do to be saved, she will not know how to respond to Christ. On the other hand, we can have the most appealing and powerful presentation of the gospel, but if we spend it on someone who has not been adequately prepared to hear and respond, our witness will fail.

Jim Petersen talks about the limitations of proclamation in his book, *Evangelism as a Lifestyle.* He argues that the apostle Paul's proclamation ministry was a unique ministry, based on a unique call, and it is not the primary style or even the most effective style for the normal Christian man or woman living at the end of the twentieth century.

Petersen's main point is that Paul worked primarily with those who had a religious heritage, who were already prepared to hear the gospel, to have the loop closed for them.[1] Petersen says that Paul's ministry, given him by God, was to "go to a city, reap those who were prepared, establish them, and move on."[2]

The strategy for those who were part of the newly established Christian communities, living in their neighborhoods and working in their cities, was quite different. Their role was to establish a relational base with their neighbors through which love could be demonstrated and trust developed. In this way, people's hearts and minds would be prepared for the proclamation of Jesus.

J. I. Packer holds a similar position. He says in *Evangelism and the Sovereignty of God,* "We have to give ourselves in honest friendship to people, if ever our relationship with them is to reach the point at which we are justified in choosing to talk to them about

Christ, and can speak to them about their own spiritual needs without being either discourteous or offensive."[3] Packer says that much of what is done today in the name of personal evangelism should really be called "impersonal evangelism," because it is mainly a distasteful invasion into the private worlds of others, an attempt to talk intimately with our neighbors before we have earned the right to do so.

Even Paul, the apostle of proclamation, knew the significance of the lifestyle in the process of evangelism. In a section of his first letter to the Thessalonians, Paul reminds them of the style of ministry that he and others carried out in Thessalonica. He says, "We were gentle among you, like a mother caring for her little children," and later, ". . . we dealt with each of you as a father deals with his own children, encouraging, comforting and urging you to live lives worthy of God, who calls you into his kingdom and glory" (1 Thess 2:7, 11-12). The Thessalonians were witnesses to the fact that Paul's life reflected the truth of what he taught. Paul says, "We loved you so much that we were delighted to share with you not only the gospel of God but our lives as well, because you had become so dear to us" (1 Thess 2:8).

The loving and caring way that the Thessalonians were exposed to the living gospel is evident in this passage. There is a proper tension here between relational and verbal evangelism. Paul and his fellow workers backed up what they proclaimed with authentic care and a deep concern that their lives would not contradict what they had to say about Jesus. They did, however, have something to say. And this takes us back to the importance of proclamation, the idea of closing the loop.

As Christians committed to cooperating with the Holy Spirit in his work of evangelism, we will concern ourselves both with our lifestyle and with the content of the Christian gospel message.

This book has by design emphasized the importance of the relational aspects of evangelism. Some have mistakenly referred to this as pre-evangelism. This shows a kind of tunnel vision, that a proclamation emphasis in evangelism is deeply ingrained in our Christian culture. A better view is to see evangelism as a long-term process of which sharing the verbal message is just one part. We need to keep this balanced perspective. If we overemphasize the importance of the verbal witness, we will tend to carry a great deal of guilt unless we are constantly and feverishly telling everyone we meet about Christ.

In the evangelism process, some prepare the soil, some plant the seeds, some weed and others water. God gives the increase and brings the repentant believer into relationship with himself. Every step of the process is significant and adds to the developing foundation on which the next block can be properly placed. This is all evangelism. No step in the process can be ignored. The seed must be planted, and the plant watered and nurtured, if there is ever to be a harvest.

We each have different gifts and will work more effectively in some aspects of evangelism than in others. Nevertheless, our aim is always to make ourselves as fully available to God as we can. We should not resist learning anything that will help us to be more effective and responsive to God's call to act in another's life.

The Message
What is the gospel message? In short, it combines several essential elements which, taken together, tell the story of how a holy but personal God has made it possible for rebellious, fallen, sinful men and women to re-establish and eternally enjoy fellowship with him through his Son, Jesus, the Savior and Lord of life.

The key here is to remember that salvation is a belief response to the person of Jesus Christ, involving our hearts, minds and wills. It includes awareness of sin and repentance, knowing the meaning of Jesus' sacrificial death and resurrection, and responding in faith to the divine call.

Christianity is not mere belief in the tenets of a theology or acceptance of a new value system. Christianity is a relationship. Our message should always lead the interested person toward this intimate encounter with Christ. Once the living relationship is established, the theological and moral aspects of the lordship of Christ naturally become important to the one who now loves Christ and wants to do what he says.

There are many biblically sound resource books with which to work if you are not comfortable enough with the message of salvation to be able to explain it simply and with impact to someone who asks you. John Stott's *Basic Christianity* or C. S. Lewis's *Mere Christianity* are two worthwhile books in this area. The following suggestions should also help.

Be a Biblical Christian

There is, of course, no better resource for us than God's own Word. By studying it, we can learn everything we need to know about the essential aspects of the gospel.

Expose yourself to Christian teaching that is centered on biblical material. Preaching, teaching, small group study and personal Bible study are all important for the normal Christian who wants to grow and learn to be more effective at sharing his or her faith and living it out in a daily context. If one of the above-mentioned opportunities for growth is not currently a part of your experience, consider adding it with regularity to your schedule. There is no substitute for God's Word.

Develop the Habit of Prayer

Perhaps nothing is more important for men and women who are serious about sharing their faith with others than being a person of prayer.

We can lean on God in prayer. We can trust him to help us see clearly how to minister most effectively to those around us. Often, when we do not know what to say or do with another, God is able to draw on our personal experience and our biblical background in such a way that we suddenly find ourselves doing or saying just the right thing when it is needed.

As we pray more, we learn what it means to hear God's voice. As we learn to trust and act upon what he says to us in prayer, we can expect to experience at deeper and deeper levels God's working through us in the lives of our neighbors.

Sharing Jesus with others is not done best as a formula. Rather it is a sensitive act that should be bathed in prayer. Every person is an individual. We seek God in this ministry to know how best to enter the life of this unique individual with whom we are working. What are the specific needs of this person? How is Christ the answer to her deepest longings? What aspect of the gospel message should be shared in this present moment? What should not be said? Should we be aggressive or gentle with this person? Should we teach about Christ or offer a touch of love in his name?

Sharing Christ with our neighbors is a complex task. We need God's help to do it right. Through prayer God will speak to us, lead us and build our understanding of the uniqueness of each person with whom we want to share the good news.

Be an Aware Christian

This book is not a book on technique, but aims at helping Christian men and women to see the world in a fresh way. This is what I mean by awareness. Being aware is learning how to live with people eyes, recognizing the opportunities that are everywhere around us to touch our world with the love of Christ. If we have the eyes to see, our world will open up for us as Christians. We will discover new ways to love our neighbor and share the goodness of God.

Awareness is also necessary if we are to pick up on the issues of sensitivity mentioned above in the paragraphs on prayer. An aware Christian will be thinking, seeing, receiving clues about the subtle realities of another's life which might be openings for or barriers to the gospel. This is necessary in order to personalize our evangelism and have the greatest effect for God.

Paul can be our example again. One need only read the brief account of Paul's proclamation to the philosophers in Athens to see how important it was for Paul to understand those with whom he wanted to share the good news (Acts 17:16-34). His work at Athens was effective because he knew his audience. We too should work to be aware of the cultural, historical and personal factors that bear on another's life to share the gospel in a penetrating way.

Know Your Own Story

Our story is a testimony to interested people about how Jesus entered our lives and became our Savior and Lord.

The story we tell of our salvation in Christ should involve the significant elements of biblical content that are a part of the gospel message. These elements are personalized in our stories so that those with whom we are sharing can see how the message touched and changed us, and can better see how it might touch and change them. Our story opens our life to another person and allows the gospel narrative to become an intimate experience which others can enter into on an emotional as well as a rational level. The gospel is personalized, made real and understandable, something a cold theological narrative could never accomplish.

Work on your story. Make it brief, but as complete as possible, well balanced, including the important biblical elements of the gospel. Fill it with the truth of the gospel, and fill it with the true emotional realities of your own experience.

Tell your story to Christian friends. Have them help you to sort out the most effective aspects from those parts of the story which might be shortened or dropped. Practice telling the story of how Jesus came into your life. Be ready to tell it to others when they ask you the reason for the hope that is in you.

There is an important reason why your story should be rooted in the truth of Scripture and in the historical facts of the death and resurrection of Christ. Remember, people involved in cults and other religions also have stories to tell about how their religious choices have changed their lives for the better. These people will be quick to share about their warm fellowship, the nice people that are in their groups, the caring they receive from others.

But Christians have more to share than the important human and social elements of church life. The gospel is based on truth. It is rooted in true history. God is alive. He is active in our lives and in his creation. Jesus, the God-man who entered our world, lived with us and died for us, rose from the dead, and is alive today. The Christian message centers on how the Savior's death deals with the problem of human sin. When we tell our story, it should include these historical realities that are foundational to faith in Christ.

The facts of our historical faith create a substantial context in which an authentic response to Jesus can best be made. We love to tell the story. But it is a story of how the real and living Christ entered our lives. It is a true story.

Let us not forget how important it is to share a word of truth with those who are lost in the rootless subjectivity of our present world.

An Unchurched Culture

Most of the men and women you will talk with about Christ have now grown up in an unchurched culture. We cannot count any longer on having a religious heritage and background that creates a bridge of understanding for our verbal message. It is increasingly important today to think of ways to express the gospel message in clear and simple language. It would be a mistake to use abstract theological terms to share the gospel today. Few in the modern world have any response to such terms as *regeneration, justification, sanctification*. These terms and concepts hold little meaning for and are confusing to men and women in our day.

It is not even a good idea to use long biblical quotes or a series of verses in our personal witness. Reading long biblical passages to those who have grown up outside of the stream of Christian thinking is like reading English to a non-English-speaking person from another country.

A better approach would be to develop the significant biblical concepts by paraphrasing key ideas in your own words and building on the key concepts with personal illustration. As interest and willingness to actually study the Bible increase, you can move into more complex material and teach it. When choosing biblical material to use in witnessing, choose short, clear verses whenever possible, and remember that you cannot assume that your neighbor now has even the slightest conceptual grasp of theology or the Bible.

We are missionaries to our own culture today. Be a student of the unchurched culture. Learn how to communicate clearly the truth of the gospel in the common language of your neighbors. Create illustrations that work today, that are meaningful to people of our times.

Style Marks for Christian Witness

Another general principle that is helpful to remember is that it will always work better to bring the Christian message to others in a loving, caring and sensitive way, rather than being judgmental and condemning. This is a lesson I learned the hard way early in my Christian life.

Judie and I were students at the University of Wisconsin when we became Christians in October during my senior year. We were excited about our new faith in Christ, and we had been witnessing to my parents who lived near us. It was about two weeks before Christmas when we heard a knock on the back door of the little house we were renting. I opened the door. My dad was there, banging the snow off his boots. He came in, sat at our table, and told us he had a very hard thing to say. He couldn't even look us in the eyes as he spoke. "We don't want you to come home this Christmas. If you're there, you'll just spoil things for the rest of us."

His words came as a complete shock. My dad is one of the most loving, gentle men I've ever known, and our family has always been close. Something dreadful had to be happening for him to face us with the news that we were not welcome at the most precious family celebration we shared. What was it?

In just two brief months between my conversion and my dad's visit, I had managed to totally alienate my entire family. My dad's words pointed out in no uncertain terms how I had failed to demonstrate to my family the newfound love I claimed.

For openers, I remember thinking that what they needed most was to know that they were going to hell. I told them this right away, for their own good. After that I made it clear that I could no longer hang around with them because their bad influence might rub off on me. And when it got closer to Christmas, I just had to let them know that the way they celebrated Christ's birthday, with drinking and gluttony, was sinful.

I can almost laugh about this today. Think of it. Everything was always fine in our family before. Then suddenly, there I was, the son my parents had poured twenty years of effort and sacrifice into, telling them that their lives really amounted to nothing and that all the family activities I had enjoyed throughout my life now showed up on my long list of mortal sins.

Fortunately Christ's love broke through. Judie and I asked if we could come over and meet with everybody a few days before Christmas. I did the first loving thing in my family since becoming a Christian. I asked my whole family to forgive me for being so incredibly arrogant and judgmental. We shared tears together. It was the beginning of a new relationship which became better than I might have ever dreamed possible. I'll never forget how my attitude and behavior hurt the people closest to me. I never want to make that same mistake again.

It seems to be so easy for us to slip into that traffic-cop mentality, condemning in our neighbors everything from smoking to dancing—and doing it in the name of Christ. I am not saying that Christians should not stand up in our day against sin. But I am saying that we should pick our battles carefully. Too often we drive wedges between ourselves and others on the basis of trivial behaviors that are not even explicitly condemned in Scripture. If we are going to chance harming a potentially fruitful relationship over an issue, the issue had better be important enough to risk losing a person for whom Christ died.

It is also important to have a sense of humor about you when you talk with others about Christ. Remember that humor is our affectionate way to share important information. Try not to be gloomy but more on the casual side. Our message is one of joy, filled with hope and light. The gospel will fall on open hearts and ears only if we can keep from putting the other person on the defensive when we talk about the things that are close to us. Once a person becomes defensive, that person stops listening. He is now busy creating his defense.

Many of the most effective Christian witnesses have developed casual phrases that can lead others into a discussion of spiritual things. I knew of one Christian man who worked concessions on the fair circuit in Colorado. He was an exceptionally good listener. Whenever he would hear someone tell of something positive happening in his life, he would say, "Oh, it sounds like the Lord is blessing you." This simple reference would often open up a fruitful spiritual exchange.

Another good way to position our witness to others is to talk about things *we* have learned rather than telling others what we think *they* need to know. It is easy for me to listen to another person talk about how he learned something significant and then to apply the insight to my own life. It is difficult for me to listen attentively to someone who has a plan for my life, who has me all figured out and wastes no time telling me what I need to know and do. Pastors whose sermons are filled with "you must" and "you should" and "you have to" unnecessarily create the same kind of communication barriers between themselves and their people. Someone has said that evangelism should always be a humble adventure, like one beggar showing another beggar where to find food.

A Proper Perspective

One thing that helped me a great deal was when I realized fully for the first time that the ultimate responsibility for evangelism lay in God's hands, not mine. I used to feel pressured to tell everyone I met about Christ. The pressure did not come from God. I felt more responsible for the salvation of my neighbors than I had any right to feel. God has made one thing clear to me. I am not the savior. I cannot save my neighbor, my child, my wife, my friend. Jesus is the only one who can do that.

Now I am much more comfortable and patient about fitting into God's timing in the evangelism process. God creates the circumstances in another's life that open the door for the good news to flow naturally. It has taken me three years as a member of the YMCA in town to build enough relationships of trust to begin to enter significantly into the lives of other members and the staff at the Y. I have not pushed, and now the doors are beginning to open wide. The same thing is true of the service club of which I am a member. It has taken two years of being a conversational friend to build relationships to the point where other men in the club have begun to let me in at the more intimate levels of their lives. It pays to be patient. Love, patience and sensitivity will reap a far greater harvest than any behaviors which grow out of the pressure we put on ourselves from a false sense of guilt or an excessive view of our own importance in the evangelism process.

Patience also requires that we resist pouring out the whole load on a person at once. Just because a friend shows some interest in

Christianity does not mean that we should quickly develop a three-hour lecture and force him or her to sit through it. It is far better to ask ourselves what piece of the puzzle can fit in here, at this moment, that will take this person just one step further. People need time to assimilate new ideas, to test them and turn them over in their minds, to decide how the new information fits in. Giving too much before people are ready to receive it will only confuse them.

Being born again spiritually is a process which has similarities to our birth into the physical world. You cannot rush the process without having negative results. When a doctor has to induce labor early, the doctor knows there is increased danger ahead. Sometimes we make this mistake in the church. We try to move someone faster than we should toward the birth event. By pushing we produce weak and struggling new Christians. With more patience and sensitivity we would allow people to mature in God's timing. When a baby is really ready to be born, nothing can stand in its way. When God adds to the church those who are being saved, a mark of authenticity will be an observable new birth energy we can in no way prevent.

Another important consideration is our long-term commitment to those with whom we share our faith. It is easy to be a dive bomber. We just swoop down, unload and disappear into thin air. But the demands of love in the evangelism process would suggest that once we choose to enter the life of another at an intimate level, uncovering hurts and hopes that are answered by the gospel, we commit ourselves to caring for and nurturing that person through the healing process. There is no room in the church for the Christians who are more concerned with how many notches they have on their Bibles than they are with nurturing those for whom Christ gave his life.

Ready to Give an Answer

Finally, be willing to do your best to answer the honest questions of those who are seeking to understand Christianity and Christ. We have a responsibility to help thoughtful and interested persons for whom certain issues and questions are a stumbling block. It is not necessary for us to have all the answers. Honest seekers will not need or demand this kind of absolute and perfect performance. The best posture is to be a co-learner with the person interested in Christianity, working out solutions to problematic issues together. This is especially effective when the search centers in the biblical material.

It is not enough today to say to thinking people, "You just have to have faith." This reinforces in them the preconceived notion they often already carry that to be a Christian means you have to throw your mind away. Write down the questions you are most often asked, and do your best to have answers which you think will help the interested seeker. Remember that it will not be our clever answers that will win people to Christ. But a good answer can help reduce the resistance. Cliffe Knechtle's *Give Me An Answer* is an excellent resource.

We also need to be aware of the fact that some people will ask questions as a smoke screen, trying to avoid the real issues of the Christian faith. This kind of person can be gently guided back to the core questions that relate to his personal life and his need for a Savior.

Judie and I had an interesting time with a middle-aged man who taught high school with me in Minnesota. Roy and I struck up a theological conversation one day in the teachers' lounge. He seemed interested in talking more, so I invited him to dinner one night the following week. I never knew anyone who could come up with so many questions about the Christian faith. We had him to dinner several times, but we were never successful in leading him any closer to a commitment to Christ. Judie realized what was happening before I did. She reminded me that Roy was a lonely single man who was starved for company and enjoyed the family atmosphere of our home. He continually thought up new and more difficult questions for us so we would keep asking him over for dinner.

Keeping someone focused on the central issues is sometimes difficult. We did not close the loop for Roy while we lived in Minnesota. But he called us during our second year in Colorado to tell us a wonderful story of how he became a Christian one evening as a former student visiting from the university shared his personal testimony with Roy. Roy said that, after he heard his friend's story, he was so moved he fell to his knees, asked Jesus to be his Savior, and wept with joy.

Closing the Loop

There is no getting around the confrontational aspect of sharing the gospel. As hard as it is for many of us to cross that final bridge and bring a friend into direct confrontation with the Lord of life, it must be done. We can and should share the truth in love. The facts about our sinful condition, God's answer to our dilemma, and the need for a personal response to the Savior, all must be shared if the person with whom we are working is to know how to make peace with God, and enter into a joyous personal relationship with Jesus Christ.

Do not shrink from sharing the good news with those you love. The apostle Paul wrote, "I am not ashamed of the gospel, because it is the power of God for the salvation of everyone who believes" (Rom 1:16). Be Christ's ambassador, taking his word of truth and love to the world. You have a precious gift of blessing to extend freely in the name of Christ.

Give it away today.

For Individuals or Groups

1. What does the author mean by his phrase "closing the loop"? How does that describe the process of adding a verbal witness to one's lifestyle witness?

2. Did the apostle Paul's proclamation ministry differ from the ongoing ministry of the churches he visited? If so, how?

Which sort of ministry are you best equipped for? Explain.

3. Can you think of examples of what J. I. Packer calls "impersonal evangelism"?

To what extent does our concern for people's souls justify our invasion of their privacy?

4. Why does the author refuse to call this a book about *pre*-evangelism?

How does he describe the evangelism process?

5. What is your story of coming to faith in Christ?

Have you ever shared your story with someone else?

Why does the author stress this aspect of one's personal story?

6. How will reading this chapter change your verbal witness for Christ?

What *will* you do if they find out you're born again?

13
Everyday Evangelism

There was a long order line at Kentucky Fried Chicken. The young woman behind the counter was obviously distressed. I watched the upset customers ahead of me fidgeting and shaking their heads. Some made critical comments to the girl as they reached the head of the line.

The restaurant was understaffed during its busy period. The backed-up orders were not the young woman's fault. I felt bad for her as I moved ahead. My mind turned to prayer.

Then I was at the head of the line. I remember smiling and saying something encouraging about the way she was handling things under pressure. I ordered as she wrote it down.

When she returned to the counter with my family's lunch, a

strange, unexpected thing happened. I was handing her the money. The young woman took it, then stopped suddenly and looked up at me. Her eyes were filled with pain. She said quietly, "I've just had an abortion."

We were total strangers. I'm certain that I would have been caught completely off guard if I had not been praying for the young woman from the first moment I noticed the difficult time she was having. I think my response was appropriate.

"No one should have to go through that alone," I said.

It only took a moment to scratch my name and number on a piece of paper. I handed it to her and asked her to call. She said she would.

For a suspended moment, there in the restaurant, I was able to share in this other person's pain. For this hurting young woman and me, it was as if time stood still. The line of angry people faded into the distance, the smell of fried chicken was gone, and God was addressing a human need.

I wish I could say that she followed through and made contact with me. She did not. Several days later I stopped back to see her. She had quit the job at Kentucky Fried Chicken and moved on. I have to trust that our brief encounter had some purpose in God's design, purpose upon which I could only speculate. It is in the hands of God.

What interested me a great deal—and this is how the story is germane to our topic—is that God was able to communicate through me something concrete about himself to this young woman, and in the most unlikely setting imaginable. All I did was order chicken—the old-fashioned recipe.

This should be an encouragement to all of us. God is able to make us the aroma of Christ in the world in almost any circumstance. If we keep this in mind, it will add excitement to every moment of our lives. What will God choose to do next in the lives of those around me, even perfect strangers? How will he use me as

I drive my car, ride with others in an elevator, stand in line at the grocery store, answer my phone or a knock at the door, strike up conversations on the bus or in the health-club hot tub, or interact with waiters or waitresses at a restaurant? If we are prayerful and expectant, God can and will use us anywhere and everywhere. But if we are not paying attention, we may miss out on opportunities to share in some wonderful, Spirit-led experiences, through which God may accomplish his work of love in another's life.

A friend of mine told me a story about her family being detained in a parking lot and having a difficult time getting the attendant to help sort out the problem. Her husband became irritated and let the attendant know in no uncertain terms how a real parking lot ought to be run. The attendant noticed their "I Found It" bumper sticker. At just the right moment he poked his head in the window and said calmly to the whole family, "Are you sure you found it?"

We are told that the prophet Daniel was received by men "because an excellent spirit was in him" (Dan 6:3 KJV). That spirit resided in Daniel because he had a deep and abiding walk with God. Daniel knew from experience that God would work in amazing and unexpected ways in the lives of his people.

What is this "excellent spirit"? How do we acquire it? How do we communicate it?

Foundational to the development of this reality is, of course, our choice to make ourselves available to God. We choose to open our lives and spirits to Jesus. We obtain an "excellent spirit" by letting the Spirit of Christ work in us, transforming our hearts, our minds, our wills.

Paul says in Romans 12:2, "Do not conform any longer to the pattern of this world, but be transformed by the renewing of your mind." There are two important things to notice about this familiar verse. First, the transformation we desire depends on our willingness to open our minds to the renewing truth and spirit of God. The more time we devote to making ourselves available to Christ and his word, the more we can expect to grow in maturity, gaining knowledge of his effective love, and attaining an "excellent spirit" through which God can accomplish his work.

Second, we are to choose changed behavior. Paul says, "Do not conform." We are to act on the truth of Christ. As we act in obedience, Jesus' personality invades our own. The excellence of his spirit matures in us. Marked with his love, we become the aroma of Christ to the world around us.

God is able to work through our words and actions to communicate Christ to the world. It is a mysterious thing, but we know from experience that the Spirit of Christ uses our normal behaviors as vehicles for the divine. We cooperate with this process by attending to the things of God and allowing God to transform us and recreate us in the image of Christ. The result of our transformation is that the aroma of Christ freely flows through our personalities and into our hurting world.

The character of Christ is most effectively carried to those near us in the things we say and do in love, joy, peace, patience, kindness, goodness, faithfulness, gentleness and godly restraint. These qualities, the fruit of the Spirit, produce fruit for God when they are rooted and grounded in God's powerful love. Our greatest hope for becoming the aroma of Christ and influencing the world around us is to pray that an authentic combination of genuine caring within and chosen loving behavior without will be found in us, God's people.

Each year on my birthday I receive a card from a used car dealer from whom I once purchased a vehicle. I am reminded annually of the emptiness of a caring behavior that is not rooted in authentic concern. A sham will not impact the world for Christ. But when our loving behaviors grow naturally out of the excellent Spirit of Christ developing within us, we will begin to observe a difference in the way men and women around us respond. The other world, the kingdom of God, in which we live and have our being, will continually make itself known through us. Our own personalties act like prisms through which the fullness of God's light and love flow. The spiritual reality of Jesus Christ is made visible to the world through the physical prism of our transformed personalities.

Writing this book has helped me to focus my attention more directly on all of life's experiences. One thing I've learned about myself is that I seem to do better in the area of witness when I'm faced with a dramatic situation that requires action. Where there is a clear moral decision to be made or an irrefutable human need, I tend to respond with integrity. And when I fail to respond in dramatic cases like these, I know with undeniable certainty that I have blown it.

The area in which I continually seem to fall short is living perceptively as a Christian in the commonplace. I often fail to see clearly with the eyes of God the possibilities that occur in the usual, everyday experiences of living. And the commonplace experiences that are the most difficult for me to view redemptively are those contemporary realities that are normally a source of personal irritation.

Telephone Evangelism

Nothing upsets me more than to receive at our evening mealtime a call from someone trying to sell something or take a survey over the phone. Supper time is the one time during a day when our family can still gather together and have fellowship and conversation. Two or three times a week I receive a call of this type during the supper hour.

My normal response to these calls has been to snap at the persons calling, saying something about their poor timing, or their invasion of my privacy. Somehow, I never really thought much about the possibility of having a positive influence in the life of one of these callers until a friend of mine told me an interesting story.

He took a call from a young woman canvassing for a local solar heating firm. He happened to be interested in looking into solar heating, and so he stayed on the phone with her. But after a short time the conversation moved to a more personal level. He found out more about her. The talk drifted to her personal financial needs. The young woman really needed a better job.

My friend was impressed with her telephone ability and manner. He recommended her to a Christian friend of his who was looking for a telephone person in his financial management firm. The young woman got the job and was quite grateful. My friend was successful in creating a place of Christian contact for this young woman. His willingness to listen created an open door for change in another's life, change that could possibly make an eternal difference.

Perhaps we could take a first step in this area by at least attempting to be polite with telephone solicitors. If we stop to think about how many calls they must make and how often they must hear a sharp remark and the sound of the receiver going dead in their ear on the other end, we can begin to imagine what a difference it might make to be treated courteously.

This area is wide open for experimentation. If someone calls at an inconvenient time for you, ask him or her to call again later. When you have a moment, pray for the person and about how the phone conversation might go when the call is returned. If you do not want to buy and are not interested in the product, honestly and politely tell the person that. But make an attempt to enter into the life of the caller if at all possible. Tell the person that you realize what a tough job it is. Ask how he or she got started in telephone sales. Having a sense of humor, laughing with these people about some of the worst experiences they've had, could open up a real opportunity for relationship. It would not be unimaginable that you might have an opportunity to invite this person to church. There may be a program at the church or an educational experience or film to suggest.

Most of us are busy. We simply do not have the time to hang on the phone with every salesperson who calls. But we might set a goal of trying to enlist one telephone salesperson a week in a meaningful conversation. If you have to narrow the field, it would be smartest to work with local people you may have some opportunity to meet in your community.

Another way we might influence others today is through our creative use of telephone answering machines. Most people I know despise these contraptions. But if you must have and use one, think of creative ways to make your opening remarks. Someone has said you cannot make a first impression a second time. How you use the beginning section on your answering machine tape can say a number of things about you, your family or your business. You can express caring to the caller. Or you can have a variety of interesting introductory segments that can make those calling you feel that they would like to get to know you in person. This is an area where Christians can be uniquely different, opening up possibilities for interaction that might not otherwise occur.

Door-to-Door Sellers

My good friend Hulda, who is now in her upper eighties, has made a lifelong ministry out of sharing the gospel with the walking mission field that finds its way to her doorstep. She prays continually that God will bring persons to her door so that she can invite them in and share with them the love of Christ.

Hulda is a delightful, bright lady. She never lies to a salesman. She lets him know right away whether she is interested in his product or not. But she always invites sellers in by saying that she will be glad to listen to their presentation if they will promise to grant her a few minutes at the end to tell them something important.

She has countless stories of how the Lord has worked miracles through her consistent ministry to these persons. Many make their presentations, hear what Hulda has to say about the Lord, share some home-baked cookies and coffee or milk, and become friends.

They stop back regularly. Hulda has in this manner been the aroma of Christ to hundreds.

Again, most of us are too busy to treat every solicitor in this thorough manner. We can, however, be polite in our dealings with people, and sincerely wish them good fortune in their work. If we can keep from feeling defensive, honestly refuse free gifts and promotions that are a part of the sales technique, stay in control of the situation on our doorstep without letting our negative emotions take over, there is a good possibility that we may influence some in a positive way.

One friend of mine has told me that he believes Christians ought to buy something from time to time, just because they are Christians and have a generous spirit of freedom regarding their money. Certainly there are real opportunities to help some of the kids who come by. We can feel good about this. We might even budget a small amount of money each month for this cause. And how do we know whether young people are giving us a line or telling about a legitimate need? We don't. But it appears that being ripped off occasionally is not inconsistent with what we know to be true about living the Christian life.

Automobile Behavior

How we drive and treat other drivers today is another good test of how seriously we believe in loving our neighbors. Both for the sake of safety and for the opportunity to be a bright spot in another's day, we should be alert and courteous drivers.

Be quick to give others the right of way at intersections. And take the time to let other drivers into your line of traffic. You know how good you feel when someone lets you in line when the traffic is dense. We can spread a lot of kindness every day by attending to these simple opportunities to let others in ahead of us. Jesus said the one who is greatest in the kingdom is the servant of all. As you are driving in your community, consider whether the other drivers around you would be happy to visit your church and meet you in person.

One Christian family I know tells numerous stories about interesting friendships they have developed with total strangers on cross-country driving trips. This family watches to see if there is another car heading their way that they see again and again. If they identify another family traveling in their direction, they wave when they pass the second or third time. Then they watch for the car at rest stops or service stations and introduce themselves with casual conversation. It is amazing to hear the stories of how often the two families will have things in common or even share mutual friends in different parts of the country. This family says they have often had natural opportunities to meet needs in the lives of others, and to share their faith.

Christians can be the first to stop and help a stranded motorist, and should respond quickly with assistance in an accident situation. If we pass by an accident site where professional help is already on the scene, we can pray for the victims of the crash. We should never underestimate the power of prayer.

Another good prayer habit to establish is to take the time to pray for other drivers we see who appear to be tense and under pressure. These drivers are often accidents just waiting to happen. Praying for, instead of fuming about, these drivers will also keep our minds and hearts in tune with the Spirit.

One morning on my way to work I pulled up behind a truck stopped at a light on a major highway leading into town. I could see that the young man driving the truck had music playing and headphones on. He was bouncing around in the cab, really enjoying the tunes. Just then I heard a siren down the road to the left. A huge fire truck was roaring up the highway toward us. At the same instant I realized that our light was in the process of turning from red to green and that the young man ahead, who was not looking to the left and not able to hear the siren because of the music, was about to pull out directly in front of the speeding fire engine.

All I could do was frantically pray and stand on the horn. I honked and honked. The young man ahead thought I was being impatient. He hesitated just long enough to turn around and give me the finger. That brief pause was enough to save his life. The screaming fire truck swished past his front bumper and zoomed on down the highway.

The young man pulled ahead, and then off to the side of the road. As I drove past he mouthed, "Sorry," when our eyes met. His face was as white as a sheet. He was visibly shaken. He was thankful to be alive.

If we drive courteously and keep an eye out for ways to help other drivers, this is another area where we can impact our contemporary world for good. I even heard of one second-mile Christian driver who liked to occasionally pay a highway toll for some stranger behind him. There is really no way to know what kind of effect this might have on another or where a giving behavior like that might lead. We can even be the aroma of Christ in the world from behind our steering wheels.

Shopping Lines and Store Personnel

Some of my most interesting experiences have come when I have simply been successful in engaging another person in conversation. Practicing the art of small talk will create open doors into other's lives that one would not imagine possible.

One time at a supermarket the man ahead of me was carrying a box with two weird-looking, long, thin things dangling out of a small slit in the lid. I could not figure out what was in the box. The things dangling out the side looked like a pair of rat's tails. So I asked the man what he had in the box. He was carrying a live lobster. Those were the lobster's antennae sticking out. Once we started talking while standing in line, we chatted about a number of things quickly which had to do with the quality of life.

After finding out that I worked at a Presbyterian church, the man told about growing up in a Presbyterian church and what a good experience it had been for him. That was a happy time in his life. He was not now attending church and felt this might be what was missing from his life. He thought he would pick a church in town and start attending again. This entire conversation transpired in less than five minutes while the two of us stood in line at the grocery store.

A woman who is on our staff at the church has had many similar experiences by keeping alert to small-talk opportunities. Jill tells me that she always tries to find something encouraging or complimentary to say to sales clerks in the stores where she shops. She says that complimenting someone on her hair or dress often opens up opportunities for further conversation that can be very fruitful.

Many of us have regular patterns in our lives that bring us into contact over and over again with the same persons, but we do not take advantage of these contacts. We shop regularly in the same store, eat in the same restaurants, buy gas at the same filling station, regularly transact business at the same bank. Often we see the same people working in these establishments almost every time we are there. It is a real mistake to neglect these regular opportunities to get to know these people better by having conversation each time we see them. We have regular opportunities to enter into their lives. If they get to know us, and through us Christ has communicated something to them of his love and care, when crisis comes into their lives, we may be the people they choose to trust and depend on for help.

A pastor friend in Illinois tells the story of one of his own life patterns of stopping a couple of times a week at the same filling station for years and having the same man come to the pumps to fill his car. Each time he drove in, Cal would just open the window a crack and say, "Fill 'er up." The only other interchange was when Cal paid the man his money through a slit in the window.

It suddenly occurred to Cal one day that he had seen this same man a hundred times or more and did not even know his name. That day when he pulled in for gas, he got out of the car and introduced himself. Each stop after that he took time to get to know the man a little more. A friendship developed.

One evening Cal received a surprise call from the man's wife. Her husband had died suddenly of a heart attack. She had no one to turn to. But her husband had so often mentioned the pastor who came by the station, that she felt he was someone to be trusted. Cal did the funeral, helped the woman through a difficult grieving time, and eventually led her to Christ. She became a faithful and energetic believer.

We have a good opportunity with people we see regularly in this way. I think especially about the waiters and waitresses in restaurants I frequent. These service persons are often ignored today or given a hard time by demanding customers. I have found that a little kindness can help establish a rapport that may lead to meaningful interaction. Just thanking your waitress, showing gratitude for her work, can build a relationship over time. Asking your waitress her name and remembering it three weeks later when you stop in again can have a surprisingly positive effect on her.

There are countless ways we can engage others. Christians should be second-mile thinkers, creative in recognizing and making use of interpersonal opportunities.

A friend of mine recently told me about flying to Europe and sitting next to a man who became curious about my friend's Scripture memory cards. He wondered what Sterritt was doing and asked him about the cards. Sterritt explained that he was memorizing the biblical material, and that the man could be a great help if he would be willing to check him on his memorization. The man agreed. Sterritt said that for the next hour he recited Scripture to this fellow who, it turned out, had many questions about the meanings of the various verses. The situation became a great opportunity for Sterritt to share the gospel with his fellow traveler.

If we commute by bus or plane, or even car pool, these circumstances often allow us to strike up conversations with those around us. We can all learn to make the most of the opportunities we have to meet new people and enter into their lives.

People Eyes

Each of us can benefit from being more focused. As Christians, it is our obligation to see the world around us perceptively, with the mind of Christ. We can pray for and receive the gift of people eyes. We can ask God for the courage to be different, to reach out and touch others when this is not the norm in our society today. As we experience the great work that God can do through us in even the most common experiences of life, we will become excited about living in this new way. Those experiences we formerly thought of as irritations and interruptions in our lives will be seen to have redemptive value if we stay alert to the quiet nudge and encouragement of God's Spirit.

And when nothing else seems possible, pray for those you see but have no opportunity to touch. Standing in a long line gives us a good opportunity to look for those around us who might seem particularly stressed or hurting. Ask God to help these persons. You may never have an opportunity to personally interact with them. But often, while you are praying, this person near you will look at you with a knowing expression in his or her eyes. God is able to comfort and touch through your authentic concern in prayer.

Life for so many in our times is a draining and difficult experience. People are hurting. They long for love. They long for a sign that someone cares about them, that someone wants to know them personally, that someone is willing to answer their need with authentic concern and practical love.

Every normal Christian man and woman today can have a major impact on our world for the cause of Christ. It does not take great expertise, exhaustive knowledge or extensive training to make a significant difference. All we need to do is to open our eyes and open our lives to those around us.

Just a touch of love today from each of us can turn the world upside-down for Christ.

For Individuals or Groups

1. What does it mean to have an "excellent spirit" (p. 136)?
How can we cooperate with the Spirit to obtain it?

2. Has someone ever showed care for you in a way that you suspected was not rooted in authentic concern? What was this experience like for you?
What should be our goal as Christians regarding the inner reality beneath our outward behavior toward others?

3. What is one common, everyday reality of life mentioned by the author in this chapter that is a possible opportunity for you to be a witness for Christ?
What might you do to develop this aspect of your life with an eye toward sharing the gospel with others?

4. What are some everyday aspects of life not mentioned by the author that could be open doors for sharing the gospel in our day?

5. What do you think it means to have the gift of "people eyes"?
How might you improve in this area?

6. What is one insight you've gained from this book that you are sure will make you a more effective witness for Jesus Christ?

7. What is one practical idea from this book that you have already put into practice in your life that has had the positive result of allowing you to enter the life of another person with the love or care of Christ?

NOTES

Chapter 2: The Risk of Love
[1] *The New York Times,* March 27, 1964.
[2] *Newsweek,* March 21, 1983.

Chapter 4: The Transparent Marriage
[1] Armand M. Nicholi II, "The Fractured Family," *Christianity Today,* May 25, 1979, p. 12.
[2] Daniel Yankelovich, "A World Turned Upside Down," *Psychology Today,* April 1981, p. 58.
[3] "Focus" (Sunday newspaper supplement), *Boulder Daily Camera,* June 1981.
[4] Yankelovich, p. 85.
[5] Ibid.
[6] Richard Selzer, *Mortal Lessons: Notes in the Art of Surgery* (New York: Simon and Schuster, 1976), pp. 45-46.

Chapter 6: New Men for a New Day
[1] Margaret Mead, *Male and Female: A Study of the Sexes in a Changing World* (New

York: Morrow, 1949), pp. 190-206.

Chapter 7: The Witness of Working Women
[1]Rita Peters, "Working People," *Innovations* (Elgin, Ill.: David C. Cook), Bonus Issue 1985, p. 32.
[2]George Gilder, *Sexual Suicide* (New York: Quadrangle, New York Times Book Company, 1973), pp. 244-46.

Chapter 9: Creative Excellence and Quality Products
[1]Udo Middelmann, *Proexistence* (Downers Grove, Ill.: InterVarsity Press, 1974), p. 25.

Chapter 10: Trusting and Being Trustworthy
[1]"Check Please," *Inc.,* June 1985, p. 24.

Chapter 11: Christians and the Abuse of Power
[1]"Intelligence Report," *Parade,* September 22, 1985, p. 18.
[2]Cheryl Forbes, *The Religion of Power* (Grand Rapids, Mich.: Zondervan, 1983), pp. 75-79.

Chapter 12: What If They Find Out You're Born Again?
[1]Jim Petersen, *Evangelism as a Lifestyle* (Colorado Springs, Colo.: NavPress, 1980), pp. 137-38.
[2]Ibid., p. 50.
[3]J. I. Packer, *Evangelism and the Sovereignty of God* (Downers Grove, Ill.: InterVarsity Press, 1961), pp. 81-82.

FURTHER READING

J. I. Packer, *Evangelism and the Sovereignty of God,* InterVarsity Press: Downers Grove, Ill., 1961. This book formulates the biblical foundation which ties together God's sovereignty, man's responsibility and the Christian's evangelistic duty. This book will help anyone interested in the theological basis for evangelism. A right understanding of God's sovereignty in evangelism both frees and empowers the normal Christian in this area.

Michael Green, *Evangelism in the Early Church,* Eerdmans: Grand Rapids, Mich., 1978. Green studies the early church's successes and weaknesses at evangelism and invites the modern church to learn from the practices of these Christians attempting to impact their world with the gospel of Christ. This is a complete treatment of evangelistic activity into the middle of the third century.

Jim Petersen, *Evangelism as a Lifestyle,* NavPress: Colorado Springs, Colo., 1980. This book emphasizes the importance of the relationship in the process of evangelism. Simply verbalizing the message is usually not enough. A good book for heightening awareness of the context in which evangelism best takes place.

Dick Innes, *I Hate Witnessing,* Vision House: Ventura, Calif., 1983. Here is a strong sociological work that will help Christians to understand what is needed to get through to people in our times. The book is excellent as a training manual, full of practical advice.

Robert E. Coleman, *The Master Plan of Evangelism,* Revell: Old Tappan, N.J., 1963.

This classic book examines Jesus' use of modeling, discipling and reproduction. This is another fine book for evangelism training.

Win and Charles Arn, *The Master's Plan for Making Disciples,* Church Growth Press: Pasadena, Calif., 1982. Strategy for evangelism is the focus of this book. The reader will learn how to form productive relationships, share his faith and make disciples of new converts. The book emphasizes the important role of the church in this process.

Rebecca Manley Pippert, *Out of the Salt Shaker,* InterVarsity Press: Downers Grove, Ill., 1979. Becky Pippert's book will motivate any reader who needs to regain a sense of excitement for evangelism. Good, practical material that can be immediately applied.

Richard Peace, *Small Group Evangelism,* InterVarsity Press: Downers Grove, Ill., 1985. This book is another good training tool with practical help for the normal Christian struggling to find her way in the ministry of evangelism. The book focuses a great deal on the small group process.

Don Posterski, *Why Am I Afraid to Tell You I'm a Christian?* InterVarsity Press: Downers Grove, Ill., 1983. This is another good, brief book on how to love people into the kingdom. It examines and presents Jesus' life as a model for modern-day evangelism.

Paul E. Little, *How to Give Away Your Faith,* InterVarsity Press: Downers Grove, Ill., 1966. This may be the king of practical help books on evangelism. Anyone interested in sharing his or her faith with others would do well to study this classic book and keep it in his library for reference.